COMMUNITY OF
UNIVERSITIES

COMMUNITY OF UNIVERSITIES

An Informal Portrait of the Association of Universities of the British Commonwealth 1913–1963

BY

ERIC ASHBY

Master of Clare College, Cambridge

CAMBRIDGE

AT THE UNIVERSITY PRESS

1963

PUBLISHED BY
THE SYNDICS OF THE CAMBRIDGE UNIVERSITY PRESS
FOR THE ASSOCIATION OF UNIVERSITIES
OF THE BRITISH COMMONWEALTH

Bentley House, 200 Euston Road, London, N.W. 1
American Branch: 32 East 57th Street, New York 22, N.Y.
West African Office: P.O. Box 33, Ibadan, Nigeria

ERIC ASHBY

1963

Printed in Great Britain at the University Press, Cambridge
(Brooke Crutchley, University Printer)

CONTENTS

Contents

FOREWORD

This is not an official history of the Association of the Universities of the British Commonwealth; it is a personal and unofficial commentary written for the Association's Jubilee Congress in 1963. I call it a portrait because it reflects the artist as well as the sitter. Its purpose is not to chronicle events but to illuminate an idea—the idea of cohesion among universities of the Commonwealth. To the best of my knowledge the facts it puts on record are correct; the interpretations I put on the facts are coloured by my own experience.

Many of the records of the Association were lost when its office was destroyed in an air raid in 1940. Miss Donne Sherwin, senior personal assistant in the Association's headquarters, skilfully pieced together a rough chronicle from the few records which remain and she prepared the appendices. It is a great pleasure to acknowledge her help; indeed some parts of this essay are little more than an expansion and ornamentation of the notes she prepared for me.

Many of the people whose names appear in these pages were, or still are, academic administrators. I found it difficult to decide what titles to give them, for many of them were professors, who then renounced their professorships to become administrators and were subsequently knighted. So I have described them simply by their names. Brief biographies of some of them are to be found in Appendix VIII.

Over the checking of facts I have had help from many

sources. Mr B. Cheeseman, Librarian at the Colonial Office, was kind enough to give me references to the Allied Colonial Universities Conference held in 1903. Several of my friends have generously read and criticized parts of the typescript; I am particularly indebted to Sir Robert Aitken, Mr T. Craig, Sir James Duff, Mr A. L. Fleet, Dr J. F. Foster, Sir Hector Hetherington, Sir Douglas Logan and Dr Thomas Loveday—all of whom have made valuable suggestions which are incorporated in the text. But for all opinions and prejudices, and for any errors which remain, I am of course responsible.

E. A.

Clare College
Cambridge, 1962

CHAPTER I

ORIGINS

THE BIRTH OF THE BUREAU

Burlington House, 1903

Each of the British universities is an autonomous corporation, immune from directives from any central authority, and in former days with no obligation, indeed no desire, to consult its sister institutions over any decision it makes. There was no sign of cohesion among the British universities until they were driven to consult together in order to secure their own advancement and to protect their own interests. This voluntary consultation is a recent development.

Consultation began in Scotland where the Commission of 1858 recommended that representatives of the four Scottish university courts should consult together to consider changes in ordinances in any of the four Scottish universities. It began in England when representatives of the struggling university colleges met at Southampton on 9 May 1887 to ask for financial aid from the government. Shortly after the Southampton meeting Lord Salisbury's ministry set up an *ad hoc* advisory committee and put into the Treasury estimates a sum of £15,000 to be distributed among university colleges approved for grant. The colleges approved for grant were University and King's Colleges, London, and the university colleges in Manchester, Birmingham, Sheffield, Leeds, Liverpool, Bristol, Nottingham, Newcastle and Dundee. The heads of these colleges were in the habit of meeting together occasionally and informally, but there is no record that they discussed anything except finance, so these meetings could not be said to have engendered much spirit of cohesion among British universities. Although Oxford and Cambridge (through the university extension system) had stimulated the foundation of some colleges, and although the University of London was sheltering all but one of them under her external degree system, there was no inclination among them, until 1910, to meet to discuss their common academic problems. They remained aloof from one another, each settling its own problems in its own way.

In the end it was the growing sense of fellowship among the universities of the Commonwealth which brought the British universities together. Evidence of this fellowship began in 1903, when a remarkable conference was held in the rooms of the Royal Society in Burlington House. It was called the Allied Colonial Universities Conference. It was organized by Gilbert Parker, Member of Parliament for Gravesend, who was —for those days—unusually familiar with the Commonwealth, for he was educated in Toronto and was at one time a writer for the Sydney *Morning Herald*. For two days he brought together representatives from thirty-one universities and colleges,[1] to discuss and to approve two resolutions: (1) 'that...it is desirable that such relations

---

[1] From six English, four Scottish, two Irish, three Australian universities; one New Zealand and one South African university; and fourteen Canadian universities and colleges. A full report of the conference is published in the *Empire Review*, VI (1903–4), 65–128. See also *The Times*, 3 July 1903, p. 10; 6, p. 8; 10, p. 9; 11, p. 13; 27, p. 11.

should be established between the principal teaching universities of the Empire as will secure that special or local advantages for study, and in particular for post-graduate study and research, be made as accessible as possible to students from all parts of the King's Dominions'; and (2) 'that a Council, consisting in part of representatives of British and Colonial Universities, be appointed to promote the objects set out in the previous Resolution'. The resolution went on to nominate a 'Committee for the constitution of the Council' which included the veteran Lord Kelvin, the High Commissioner for Canada (Lord Strathcona), James Bryce, R. B. Haldane, the President of the Royal Society (William Huggins), Michael Foster, the Vice-Chancellor of Cambridge and the Pro-Vice-Chancellor of Oxford, the Principal of London (Arthur Rücker) and Oliver Lodge. The resolutions were approved after two days of somewhat platitudinous speeches. Notwithstanding the wording of the first resolution, the impression created by many speakers was that the British universities had everything to give, and the 'colonial' universities everything to learn, from contact with one another. The English delegates tended to be condescending and paternal toward the 'colonial' universities, and the 'colonial' delegates tended to display a naïve filial piety toward the English universities; except for the Vice-Chancellor of McGill University, who courteously pointed out that in some subjects (mining, for instance) British students might well migrate for post-graduate study to Montreal; and for the Principal of London, who reminded the audience that it would be of little use for colonials to know something of England 'unless the average Englishman also knows something of the Empire beyond the seas'.

However, three clear ideas emerged from the conference: the first, that scholarships should be established for the interchange of graduate students among Commonwealth universities (an idea which was not fully worked out until 1960); the second, that there ought to be a 'close intimate relationship' between the universities of the Commonwealth 'which will lead to circulation of the teaching staff'; and the third, that there should be 'an organization under which the universities of the British world could associate themselves for certain forms of joint action'.

The conference ended buoyantly with a grand dinner at the Hotel Cecil, over which the Prime Minister presided and which was attended by over 400 guests, and there was talk of another conference in two years' time. But nothing came of this and nothing more appears to have been done to promote cohesion among Commonwealth universities until 1909. In November of that year the Senate of the University of London adopted a resolution: 'that it is desirable to hold an Imperial Universities Conference in London in 1911'.[1] The idea came from a discussion which the Principal of the University at that time (Henry Miers) had with one or two of his colleagues. He consulted the Vice-Chancellors of Oxford and Cambridge and with their approval an invitation to take part in an Imperial Conference was sent to all other universities in the United Kingdom. It

[1] It was in fact held in 1912.

received their unanimous approval. It was agreed that the vice-chancellors of the home universities should form a committee to take charge of the academic side of the programme. This committee met for the first time on 19 November 1910 in the offices of the University of London at South Kensington.[1] It was a red-letter day in the history of Commonwealth universities, for out of that meeting grew the Congress which gave birth to the Association of Universities of the British Commonwealth.

The first Congress, 1912

The Home Universities Committee which met for the first time in 1910 to organize the first Congress of Universities of the Empire was primarily what we should now call a working party. Similar working parties met in Australia, Canada, and India. From these meetings, and from individual universities, came suggestions for the agenda for the Congress, and the Home Universities Committee in November 1911 was able to decide on a programme. The preparations were clouded by the death in 1911 of R. D. Roberts, who was organizing secretary for the Congress. His place was taken at short notice by Alex Hill (Principal of University College, Southampton) who devoted most of the rest of his life to the cause of Commonwealth universities. He, with the aid of numerous committees, completed the arrangements. There was a very full agenda of papers and discussions. To occupy the leisure moments of the delegates a Reception Committee prepared an impressive array of entertainment including a government

[1] A list of those invited to the meeting is given in Appendix 1.

lunch, dinners by City Companies, scientific exhibits, music, and a torchlight tattoo and mimic assault entitled 'The Storming of the Sultan's Palace at Tlemcen', mounted by the University of London Contingent of the Officers' Training Corps. There was also a giant Conversazione with 2000 guests, illuminated by Japanese lanterns. It makes one a little nostalgic to read that the caterers' estimate for refreshments at this Conversazione was about 1*s*. 3*d*. per head. Both before and after the Congress tours were arranged to other universities, where delegates were entertained by orations, sermons, banquets, receptions, convocations for the award of honorary degrees, and visits to laboratories. The University of London, as so often in its history, acted as host and undertook the chief financial responsibility. The Congress received a royal benediction when the Presidency was accepted by H.R.H. Prince Arthur of Connaught. Invitations were sent to fifty-one universities, all of which sent delegates to the Congress.[1] The months of preparation were brought to a triumphant conclusion on 2 July 1912 when the Earl of Rosebery and Midlothian, Chancellor of the Universities of London and Glasgow and Rector of the University of St Andrews, opened the first session of the Congress.

Round the family hearth

The proceedings of the first Congress were published in a volume of 464 pages.[2] The most unfamiliar feature of this volume is its price—ten shillings. For the rest,

[1] A list of the universities is given in Appendix II.
[2] *Congress of the Universities of the Empire, 1912: Report of Proceedings*, ed. Alex Hill (University of London Press, 1912).

the reader in 1963 cannot escape the conclusion that however much progress universities have made in the last fifty years, the topics their representatives like to talk about have not changed. A catalogue of the sessions held in 1912 discloses how perennial (and how meagre) is the repertoire for conferences on higher education. The topics seem timeless; the voices only have changed: specialization among universities; reciprocal recognition of courses for post-graduate degrees (when J. J. Thomson and Ernest Rutherford took part in the discussion); interchange of university teachers with special emphasis on the need for university teachers in Britain to go on secondment to colonial universities; residential facilities in universities (with a brilliant contribution from Patrick Geddes, who suggested for the University of London a 'collegiate city' in Chelsea); university equivalents and mutual recognition of entrance requirements—that dreary perennial; university extension work (with contributions from Temple and Mansbridge); the place of technical and professional education in universities; representation of teachers in university government. Indeed the only item on the agenda in 1912 which would seem out of place in 1963 was one on the position of women in universities, where the discussion—as if to demonstrate that even in those days there was nothing much to discuss—was unbelievably prim and trite.

It is not merely the titles of the discussions held in 1912 which might just as appropriately appear at a Congress in 1963: many of the things which were said then are still relevant. There was the question of the function of the five new universities founded since the turn of the century. 'There has', said the Vice-Chancellor of Manchester University, 'been a striking increase of late years in the number of institutions providing a University training...' and he went on to describe the dilemma, that on the one hand, in the interests of economy, not every university should teach every subject, and on the other hand 'no outside body can lay down rules [about the allocation of subjects among universities] which might not have the effect of strangling useful and often most fruitful developments'. There was the question of academic salaries: Charles Waldstein reminded the delegates that the leading German professors were paid more than cabinet ministers or judges, while in Britain 'the remuneration for the highest intellectual services is decidedly the lowest among all liberal professions'. There were three practical plans, complete with dates and financial estimates, for the interchange of British and Australian professors. There was vigorous talk even about the two cultures, with protagonists on either side as emphatic, if not as waspish, as Snow and Leavis.

All who attend congresses know that the formal sessions, though they are as necessary as are the cutlery and glasses at a dinner party, are only instruments to facilitate the informal conversation and the unpremeditated argument which alone make these occasions worth while. And it is clear, when one reads between the lines of the four hundred pages of official talk, that in the corridors of the University of London and in the wide streets of South Kensington (in those days comparatively free from traffic) a web of understanding was being spun between the universities represented there. The delegates felt (as the Vice-Chancellor of McGill put it) 'like children gathering round the family hearth'. 'Federation', as R. B. Haldane said on another academic occasion, 'rests upon sentiment'. Any formal manifestation of federation 'can never be more than what you may call a constitutional clothing of a reality which is a sentiment'. By the end of the week the necessary sentiment had been generated and the delegates were ready to put on some constitutional clothing. It was on the morning of Friday, 5 July, at a meeting presided over by Lord Strathcona, that G. R. Parkin (Organizing Representative of the Rhodes Scholarship Trust) presented a paper on 'The Establishment of a Central Bureau: its Constitution and Functions'.[1] 'Engaged in a common task', he said, 'the Universities lack the means for common and concentrated effort, for the comparison of experience, and for the ready exchange of ideas.' To remedy this deficiency he proposed that a Bureau 'should be created by the universities themselves and remain under their exclusive control'. For the initial activities of the Bureau Parkin proposed that it should publish a Yearbook; act as a clearing house for academic appointments, for the exchange of professors, and for the exchange of students; and facilitate a study of such problems as the achievement of a common matriculation standard and a rational pattern of specialization among the universities of the Commonwealth. There was no opposition. Three Australian delegates spoke in

[1] *Congress of the Universities of the Empire, 1912*, p. 309.

favour of Parkin's proposals and the session closed. That same afternoon the delegates met privately. Donald MacAlister (Principal of Glasgow) was put into the chair.

I am quite sure [he said]...that we have formed many valuable links between the representatives of the different Universities of the Empire during these days. It is desirable that they should not be temporary only, but permanent. It is in order that we may devise some means of making them permanent that we are called together this afternoon, to invent an organ for the purpose of continuing that communication of knowledge and comparison of varied experience which has been the object of the gathering in which we have taken part.

Then Parkin, who was undoubtedly the midwife for the Bureau, spoke again, and it was resolved (*inter alia*) that congresses of the universities of the Empire should be held every five years and that 'a Committee of this Congress be now appointed to take steps for the formation in London of a Bureau of Information for the Universities of the Empire'. The Committee was to have fourteen members, seven to be nominated by the Home Universities Committee (which had organized the Congress) and seven to be nominated by overseas universities, with the following distribution: Canada, two; Australia, one; New Zealand, one; the Cape, one; India, one; and one from 'other parts of the Empire'. Before the Congress dispersed the seven members to represent overseas universities were appointed. They were: R. A. Falconer and H. M. Tory for Canada; W. H. Bragg for Australia; J. W. Joynt for New Zealand; Thomas Holland for India; and N. Tagliaferro (Malta) for 'other parts of the Empire'.[1] Subsequently the Home Universities Committee decided upon a geographical distribution for representation in the United Kingdom— a decision which was, as it turned out, to cause a good deal of trouble—as follows: Oxford, Cambridge and London: one member each; one member from the four Scottish universities; one from the five Northern universities; one from the universities of Wales, Birmingham and Bristol; and one from the Irish universities. There followed correspondence over some months with the British universities, and eventually six representatives were appointed; Donald MacAlister from Glasgow, Isambard Owen from Bristol, Michael Sadler from Leeds, Henry Miers from London, H. T. Gerrans from Oxford, and R. H. Scott from Cambridge. Alex Hill acted as honorary secretary. No representative was nominated from Ireland.

GROWING PAINS

Representation

This was the first of the growing pains. St Andrews, Aberdeen, and Edinburgh were content to have the Principal of Glasgow as their representative; Birmingham and Wales were content to have the Vice-Chancellor of Bristol as theirs. In Ireland there were three universities: the University of Dublin (Trinity College), the National University, and Queen's University, Belfast. It was suggested that the first representative of these three should be the Provost of Trinity College, the

---

[1] *Congress of the Universities of the Empire.* Friday, 5 July 1912. Afternoon Session. Confidential [Report] for the Use of Delegates only. 1912.

formidable and irascible Anthony Traill. The response
to this invitation was a broadside from the Provost
himself: 'We are unanimous', he wrote to Alex Hill on
12 October 1912, 'in saying that we claim to be recog-
nized on all such Committees as you mention, singly,
and next to Oxford and Cambridge. This procedure has
always been given us hitherto, and we decline to be
mixed up with the other two Universities in Ireland.' He
was totally unimpressed by the reply that the four
Scottish universities were content to send only one
representative to the Committee. Traill's attitude, not
unnaturally, prejudiced the other two Irish universities
against him as their representative. Hamilton, the Vice-
Chancellor in Belfast, would have been content to
nominate Traill anyway but (as he wrote to the Secretary of the Formative Committee in London): 'Nixon [at
the National University] tells me his university has not
considered favourably the nomination of Traill, who,
entre nous, bald-headedly *claims* the seat on the Committee.' Three years later the Annual Report of the
Bureau for 1915 reports laconically: 'Ireland is still
unrepresented on the Committee', and it was not until
1921 that the dispute over representation from Ireland
was resolved.

Apart from this tribal contretemps the Bureau made a
good start. Its first meeting was held in January 1913.
Donald MacAlister was elected Chairman. Alex Hill
served as honorary Secretary. It was decided to name
the infant 'The Universities Bureau of the British
Empire', to publish a *Yearbook*, to appoint corres-
pondents in each member university to feed the Bureau

with news, and to collect information on vacancies in academic staff. It was decided also that the Bureau—since it was to be entirely in the hands of member universities—would have to collect £1500 a year from its members to meet running expenses.

As soon as an appeal for subscriptions was made it became evident that not all universities were equally enthusiastic about the venture. The Committee asked for £50 a year from the bigger universities and £25 a year from the smaller ones. Cambridge pleaded that its finances were 'in a parlous condition' and declined to subscribe (although within a year it reversed that decision). Sheffield declined to contribute. By the outbreak of war there were still five member universities which had neither given nor promised subscriptions. The truth of the matter was that not all university governing bodies were prepared to support the decisions made by their representatives at the Congress. The very powerful tradition of individualism among our universities naturally made some of them a little querulous at the appearance of a body which might try to co-ordinate them or regiment them into any pattern of conformity, or even impose upon them the obligation of belonging to a community. There were many signs of this. Even before the birth of the Bureau in 1912 Liverpool and Manchester insisted that its activities must be limited to the collection and dissemination of information; and at the first meeting it was decided 'that it will at no time be the business of the Bureau Committee to pass judgement on University policy'.

Information

Even the collection of information had its dangers: some universities, for instance, objected to any disclosures about their incomes being included in the *Yearbook*; and there was a very sharp allergy toward the honorary Secretary's enthusiasm for information. The first inquiry, started even before the Bureau was set up, was to be about halls of residence. A draft questionnaire was sent to Sadler (then Vice-Chancellor of Leeds) whose comment was: 'The draft of the schedule of inquiries about the maintenance of residences for students has just reached me. May I implore you not to send it out? It would involve an enormous lot of trouble to fill up....' And four days later Sadler wrote again on a similar matter: 'The number of questions and the range of the inquiry had startled our staff.' One cannot but sympathize with Sadler. The questionnaire (or some modification of it) was in fact sent out, and the results were published in a fantastic (and fascinating) document[1] which gives, for thirty halls of residence which remain anonymous, not only information about cost, working expenses, fees, and management, but vivid details about diet and discipline. Thus Hall 1 (a women's hall) offered for breakfast tea, coffee, toast, brown and white bread, butter, choice of (generally four) meats, stewed fruit, vegetarian dish or porridge, jam, honey, marmalade; while Hall 22 offered only porridge, fish *or*

[1] *Universities Bureau of the British Empire.* Returns of information from Halls of Residence and Hostels of the United Kingdom. (No date, but known to be 1913.)

eggs, rolls, bread and butter, tea. Hall 21 had not only three meals a day, but a supper consisting of cold meat, hot minced meat, potato pie, milk puddings, cheese, bread and butter, hot milk and cocoa; while other halls offered only a glass of milk. Under discipline there are reports from all halls on 'the relations between men and women'. Hall 3 says primly that men and women may meet freely in College but 'they may not *walk* together out of College'. Another hall 'does not restrict the private conduct' of its members, and relies on informal censure to maintain propriety between the sexes. In Hall 23 'association of men and women students is not discouraged if within the knowledge of the Superintendents', and in Hall 28 (a women's hall) 'Residents are not allowed to receive gentlemen friends in their rooms (fathers excepted)'. This—its first publication— is a vivid reminder that even though the Bureau is only fifty years old, it was born in another age.

From the time of its formation in 1912 to the outbreak of war in 1914 the Bureau's Formative Committee met four times. It published, in March 1914, the first edition of the *Yearbook* (a thousand copies at a price of 7s. 6d. each). It rented for £25 a year a room in the Imperial Institute at South Kensington, and it appointed a part-time assistant secretary at a salary of £300. It optimistically proposed to circulate each week information about academic vacancies. Its overseas members were anxious for it to flourish: in May 1914 J. W. Barrett (who later became Chancellor of Melbourne University) wrote to the honorary Secretary encouraging the Bureau to advertise the services it provided. 'We should aim', he wrote, 'at making the Bureau the Mecca of every University man in the Dominions.' On 27 July 1914 a circular went out announcing that a second Congress would be held in 1917. On 7 August Donald MacAlister postponed the Committee's next meeting 'until conditions are more favourable', and the shadow of war fell across the universities of the Commonwealth.

THE POST-WAR CHALLENGE

Planning for peace

That the Bureau survived the war of 1914–18 is due to the energy and devotion of Alex Hill. Although he was Principal of the University College of Southampton, he spent two days a week in London on the Bureau's business, which he managed with the help of a lady clerk. Further editions of the *Yearbook* were produced in 1915 and 1916–17; and the Bureau undertook the singular and somewhat inappropriate task of distributing to overseas universities propaganda prepared by the Foreign Office, 'on the origin of the war, the responsibility for it of the Central Powers, and the inhumanity of the enemy's methods of warfare'.[1]

But already by 1917 Britain had begun to plan for peace. In May 1917 a Conference of British universities was called under the Bureau's auspices 'to consider the situation arising out of the closing of the German and Austrian universities to graduate students from the countries of the Allies'. Some twenty-one universities

---

[1] A large number of institutions, including a dozen universities, the Headmasters' Conference, the Association of Headmistresses, and the Bureau, co-operated with the Central Committee for National Patriotic Organizations in this activity.

and colleges were represented. The Principal of Glasgow, Donald MacAlister, was put into the chair. It was at this Conference that the idea was discussed of awarding a doctorate in British universities, as a means of attracting to Britain post-graduate workers from overseas. The Conference was adjourned so that delegates could secure the views of their universities about this revolutionary proposal. It met again a year later, on 10 May 1918, when seventy-one people were present, including representatives from universities in Australia, Canada and New Zealand. This meeting was crucial in the history of British higher education; before the Conference adjourned it had reaffirmed and commended to the universities 'as a basis for common action' the desirability of establishing the Ph.D. degree; it had resolved to co-operate with the government over sending a mission to the United States to confer with representatives of American universities; and it had agreed 'that the Vice-Chancellor or Principal of each university, or a deputy appointed by him, together with the Executive Committee of the Universities Bureau, be appointed a Standing Committee to consider any matters of common interest arising out of the proceedings of this Conference or submitted to it by the government, and to report from time to time to the Conference'. Thus on 10 May 1918, under the auspices of the Bureau and in what became known as the 'Standing Conference', the British universities entered the field of post-graduate education; they made the first common gesture of co-operation with the universities of the United States; and they agreed to set up the body which became the Committee of Vice-Chancellors and Principals.

These momentous decisions were not made without some inspiration from outside the universities. The inspiration came from A. J. Balfour. As soon as the United States entered the war, Balfour went to Washington as head of the British mission to arrange Anglo-American co-operation. He was an imaginative statesman who saw the need for Anglo-American co-operation not only to win the war but to secure the peace, and he conceived the idea that American post-graduate students should, after the war, be attracted to British universities instead of to Germany (which had been the 'finishing school' for both British and American scholars and scientists since the 1880's), and that this could best be done by strengthening our research schools and by instituting a Ph.D. degree.[1] There had clearly been some informal discussion about this before the Bureau's Conference in May 1917. But on 14 March 1918 (a week before the great German offensive was launched against the British Fifth Army) Balfour wrote to the universities a letter of such historical importance that it is worth presenting here:[2]

During my recent visit to America I was more than once consulted about the possibility of establishing closer connections between the American Universities and our own,

[1] It has been estimated that in the 1880's over two thousand Americans were studying in German universities; and ever since 1861 Ph.D. degrees, modelled on the German prototype, have been awarded in American universities. The first American Ph.D. to be awarded was in Yale (1861). By 1918 no fewer than 562 American Ph.D.'s were being awarded annually (Brubacher and Rudy, *Higher Education in Transition*, 1958, p. 188).

[2] The text reproduced here is taken from a draft sent to the Secretary of the Bureau. In paragraph 4 of the letter the date and time of the meeting were omitted. On the following day a stencilled notice was circulated giving date and time for the meeting; these are inserted in square brackets.

both by the interchange of students and teachers, by the exchange of information as to curricula, fees, terms and subjects of study, and by other methods. I have little doubt that there exists in the United States a real desire for greater intellectual intercourse with Great Britain, especially in the higher branches of University work where hitherto the influence of Germany has been unduly predominant.

At the same time there appeared to be, rightly or wrongly, an impression that there exists among British Universities, as compared with German or French, a degree of local independence and variety, combined with a lack of any common organisation or even meeting ground for consultation, which made it very difficult for Americans who might desire to finish their studies abroad to find out what work was being done in Great Britain and what University could best provide for their needs.

Of course I do not pretend to judge of the soundness of these criticisms or of the answers that may be made to them, but they are reinforced by many proposals and enquiries which have come to me at the Foreign Office from France, Russia, and other Allied countries.

The whole matter appears to me to be of such importance that, after consulting with my friend the President of the Board of Education, and hearing from him that the Board is already interested in the matter and that the English Universities are actively considering it, I am venturing now to invite representatives of all the Universities of Great Britain and Ireland to meet Mr Fisher and myself at the Foreign Office on [9 May at 3 p.m.] and confer upon the whole subject.

For example, the representatives might be willing, either directly or by means of a Committee, to consider the possibility—

(1) Of improvements in the means of collecting and disseminating the sort of information about the several Universities which is needed by a foreigner wishing to study in Great Britain;

(2) Of facilitating interchange of students and teachers;

(3) Of establishing between the Universities themselves some permanent organ of communication and consultation, and, if need be, even of common action in matters of common University interest, which could enter into relations with the similar bodies which already exist in some of the Allied Countries.

I need hardly say that both Mr Fisher and myself regard the independence and complete freedom of the Universities as a matter of the very highest importance, and should not think of proposing for your consideration any step that pointed, however remotely, towards State control.

I trust that it may suit your convenience to be present and to bring with you another representative of your university.

This meeting in the Foreign Office was a significant moment in our university history. Among those present were Balfour himself (as Foreign Secretary), the President of the Board of Education (H. A. L. Fisher), the Secretary for Scotland, the Chief Secretary for Ireland, and two representatives from each of the eighteen universities of the United Kingdom. Balfour explained that he was anxious 'not merely to fill the gap inevitably made by the exclusion of Germany from the place she had hitherto occupied in advanced teaching and in the promotion of research, but also to strengthen the higher intellectual bonds' which united Britain with her Allies. He reminded the Conference that British universities were weak in post-graduate work and it was desirable that more attention should be devoted to it. Then he went on to make a point which has profoundly influenced the British university system. Common action among British universities (he said) is difficult owing to the extraordinary variety in their history and character. He rejoiced that they had not been moulded by the State. It was, however, desirable that some machinery should be found through which the great body of university institutions could speak on occasion with a common voice. In Paris or in Rome, university feeling had this opportunity of expression, whereas the President of the Board of Education is not Minister of Public Instruction for the whole country in the continental sense. He went on to say he would like to see the tentative efforts at common expression, which began in 1912 with the foundation of the Universities Bureau, extended. As the universities increased in importance the need for a common mechanism of expression would become more and more apparent.

There and then the Conference at the Foreign Office endorsed the proposal to encourage post-graduates from the United States and other Allied countries to attend British universities; it accepted the invitation to send an academic delegation to the United States; and it adopted the following resolution:

That this Conference considers it desirable in the interests of the Universities and of the nation that steps should be taken for promoting greater co-ordination and power of mutual consultation among the Universities of the United Kingdom, whether by forming Standing Committees of the Universities, or by developing and extending the powers of the Bureau of Universities of the Empire, or otherwise, and commends this question to the consideration of the Conference which is to meet tomorrow.

It was on the next day, 10 May, that the momentous adjourned Conference of universities was held. It seems, therefore, that the creation of the Committee of Vice-

Chancellors and Principals was precipitated by A. J. Balfour at a meeting at the Foreign Office called to discuss the strengthening of post-graduate work and the institution of a Ph.D. degree in order to divert to Britain that traffic in scholars and scientists which before the war had gone to Germany. There were, of course, currents of thought flowing in the same direction in the universities themselves; indeed the Principal of University College, Reading—W. M. Childs—had made a similar proposal as early as 1912 (see chapter III), but it was at the Foreign Office that the moment of crystallization occurred.

The adjourned Conference received the proposals very cordially. It was evident from the discussion that a majority of universities were willing to institute a Ph.D. degree to be awarded to a graduate after two years of research. It is difficult to realize that although this discussion took place only forty-five years ago it was (as Ernest Rutherford said at the Conference): 'an entire innovation. It will involve a full period of post-graduate training, introducing into Britain a system practically identical with that which obtains in America.... It will be a real and very great departure in English education, the greatest revolution, in my opinion, of modern times.' Six years later, at the Home Universities Conference in 1924, the purpose in Balfour's mind was very clearly stated by another philosopher, A. N. Whitehead.

We wanted to promote the unity of our culture by providing in the Universities of Great Britain something which could be understood because of its uniformity, even of nomenclature, in every country which looks in any way to Great Britain as a centre of culture. That is the point from which the whole matter started, and in that way we revived—or, rather, we hope to revive—one of the best institutions of the Middle Ages, the wandering scholar.

If Balfour, Rutherford and Whitehead were to be confronted with the annual crop of Ph.D. theses from British universities they might have some doubts as to whether the new degree has been an unmixed benefit to higher education. But the chief by-product of the new degree—the Committee of Vice-Chancellors and Principals—has abundantly fulfilled Balfour's hope that the British universities would establish a 'common mechanism of expression'; and the arrangements, described on page 84, which bring post-graduates to British universities from the United States and the Commonwealth each year, have abundantly fulfilled Whitehead's hope: British universities now lie on the highway of wandering scholars.

An office and a constitution

The annual income of the Bureau, derived almost entirely from the subscriptions of member universities, fell from £591 in 1914 to £210 in 1918. Clearly it could not play its part in fulfilling the aspirations of the Universities' Conference of 10 May without better financial backing than this. Accordingly the Bureau's Committee decided to appeal for some support from public funds. In a draft 'Statement of Needs' signed by Donald MacAlister in December 1918 the Committee outlined its achievements since 1912 and asked for £2000 a year to defray the cost of a full-time secretary (at £800 a year) and the expenses of running a small office. It appears that the final appeal to the Treasury did not take this form, for in the following April MacAlister, writing from the Athenaeum Club (which even in those days served as a hatchery for academic schemes) mentioned that he had consulted Fisher (of the Board of Education), William McCormick (Chairman of the newly created University Grants Committee), and Lord Curzon (who was then acting as Foreign Secretary) about the possibility of a non-recurrent government grant of £5000 to acquire 50 Russell Square as a base of operations for the Bureau. The house was on the market and next door to premises which were being acquired for an American educational bureau. A formal application was made on 11 April. There was the familiar stalling: Fisher was reported to be 'not very encouraging'; he thought the Foreign Office would be more likely to help than the Board of Education.[1] McCormick suggested that the purchase might be financed from the general Treasury grant to universities. But (as MacAlister wrote later in April) 'vacillation is the prevailing temper just now. Lord Curzon remains dumb, though I have sent him a reminder.' By 3 May the chance of securing the house seemed to be slipping away. To play for time MacAlister even offered a personal guarantee of £1 a day till the end

[1] In a letter to Alex Hill dated 14 April, Fisher wrote, 'I do not think I can hold out hope of any direct grant....It occurs to me, however, that the increased Grants which the universities will be receiving this year may allow them to give the Committee such assistance as it needs or that the Advisory Committee on University Grants which is shortly to be set up, may find it possible to make a contribution out of the Parliamentary moneys placed at their disposal...' (H. A. L. Fisher to A. Hill, 14 April 1919).

of May, to keep the option open. But on 6 May there was a break in the clouds. The Board of Education, through McCormick's good offices, agreed to give £5000 to enable the Bureau to secure a base for its work. Two conditions were attached to the offer, namely that the Bureau (which had survived since 1912 without any constitution or legal expression of its existence) should become a corporation capable of holding property, and that the universities should, out of their own funds 'which the government places at their disposal', make adequate provision for the Bureau's maintenance. It is note-worthy that this latter wise condition, which safeguarded the Bureau against any criticism that it might become a government agency not under the control of the member universities, came from the Board of Education and not from the academics on the Bureau's Committee!

The decision to accept the grant of £5000 with the conditions attached to it, and to use some of the money to purchase a ten-year lease of 50 Russell Square, had to be taken by the Chairman and Secretary, MacAlister and Hill. They asked the Standing Conference, which met on 23 May 1919, to ratify their action. The Conference 'accepted with satisfaction' the government's offer and the representatives present agreed to recommend to their Councils that each university in Britain should contri-bute £100 a year toward the expenses of the Bureau. It was assumed that overseas universities, too, would subscribe. To meet the government's other condition, it was agreed that the Bureau should be incorporated under the Companies Act. It was agreed, too, to occupy 50 Russell Square. All was now clear for the Bureau to discharge its new responsibilities, though the Licence of Incorporation was not granted until 18 September, and on 23 September Hill was still urging Fisher to have a moiety of the £5000 paid to the Bureau. (The government would not pay the whole of it over until the universities had guaranteed to maintain the Bureau; the balance of the grant was not paid over until 25 February 1920, and even then only through the importunity of the newly formed University Grants Committee.) On 31 October 1919 the Executive Committee of the Bureau met at 50 Russell Square, its first real home.

CHAPTER II

CONSOLIDATION AND CONFIDENCE, 1920–60

FROM COMMITTEE TO ROYAL CHARTER

Aims and objects

From 1913 to 1919 the Bureau was a 'federation founded on sentiment' without any defined aims and objects or any formulated constitution. It could not, in this legally naked condition, enter into its post-war responsibilities. We have already seen how, as a condition of receiving a non-recurrent government grant, the Bureau had to become registered under the Companies Act. Its first Memorandum of Association, approved by the Bureau Committee in July 1919, contains a clear statement of its aims and objects. They were: to collect and distribute information of interest to universities, to arrange conferences and congresses and to facilitate interchange of information between universities and governments, to facilitate the interchange of students and teachers, to maintain a London office which should serve as a secretariat for the Committee of Vice-Chancellors, to publish handbooks, periodicals, and leaflets, to invite and collect subscriptions. The other condition was that the running expenses of the Bureau should be met from contributions from its member universities. At the Standing Conference of Universities on 23 May 1919, the delegates agreed to ask each British university to contribute £100 a year for three years towards the cost of running the Bureau. Just as the delegates were getting up to leave it occurred to the Chairman and the Secretary that it would be useful to have a paper on the aims and objects of the Bureau, and the opportunities now opening before it, to put in front of delegates to a special meeting of the Conference, to be held on 18 July, when visitors from the Commonwealth and the United States were expected to be present. Ramsay Muir (who was a member of Sadler's Commission on Calcutta University), Gregory Foster and Alex Hill were constituted a sub-committee to prepare this paper. Muir (having more time than the others) was asked to draft it.

This apparently non-contentious assignment led to one of those silly squabbles which serve as a useful reminder that academic distinction is not inconsistent with human frailty. Muir produced an eloquent—if somewhat inaccurate—essay setting out the three areas of opportunity before the Bureau: as a secretariat to the Vice-Chancellors' Committee over national questions, as a centre of cohesion for higher education in the Commonwealth, and as a headquarters for international co-operation among universities. He went on to make the point that the present machinery for managing the Bureau would be inadequate for the functions it would be called upon to perform, and that in place of the Committee there should be a Council containing representatives of all member universities, together with representatives from contributing governments (i.e. from India, Canada, Australia, etc.), and that the responsibility for managing the Bureau's affairs should be in the hands of a President, Treasurer and Executive elected annually by this Council, together with a highly paid full-time secretary aided by an adequate staff; the whole operation to cost some £10,000 a year.

In retrospect, these suggestions from Muir, which were supported by Foster, seem modest and reasonable enough; but they incensed the third member of the Committee, Hill. Hill took the view that the Committee had been asked to prepare a paper for the July Conference merely on aims and objects of the Bureau, specially for the information and encouragement of overseas visitors. Muir's draft went beyond the Committee's term of reference: it involved a complete metamorphosis of the constitution of the Bureau, and this was a matter which could not be discussed except at a quinquennial Congress. Hill was doubtless technically correct, but as one reads the angry exchange of letters between Muir and himself one cannot help feeling that the technical objection covered a disinclination on Hill's part to see the Bureau become more formal and professionalized. Muir offered to come from his home in Buxton to discuss the draft; Hill refused to meet him. Hill, who had not kept copies of some of his more astringent handwritten letters, asked Muir to return them so that copies could be made; Muir retorted by asking for his handwritten letters to be returned too. For the Conference on 18 July Muir's draft was printed (but not circulated to members beforehand) with a note at the end: 'Dr Alex Hill, who was also appointed a member of the Committee, does not concur in this Report.'[1]

[1] *Report of a Committee appointed by a Conference of British Universities to draw up a Statement on the future work of the Universities Bureau of the British Empire*... (no date).

The Conference, doubtless mystified that such a bland document should arouse such bitterness, was persuaded to remit the Report to a committee, with the job of preparing comments to be discussed at the next Conference. It is interesting to note that the Committee included a professor of English from Sydney, E. R. Holme, and such distinguished names as Rutherford and Hartog. Notwithstanding this squabble, confidence in the Bureau grew. It produced another *Yearbook*; by November 1919 it had secured promises from all the British universities to contribute £100 a year for three years; and the Secretary was directed to issue invitations for a second Congress in 1920 (the date was subsequently changed to 1921).

A Royal Charter?

Meanwhile the paper on 'aims and objects' continued to occupy the time and try the temper of the Secretary, Alex Hill. On an interleaved copy of Muir's unacceptable document he wrote in pencil a new version, summarizing the history of the Bureau, incorporating some of Muir's passages about the new opportunities open to it as the 'headquarters of the diplomatic and consular service of the British universities', and giving examples of the services it had already performed. He polished up this draft and circulated it to the Committee, for consideration at a meeting to be held on 24 March 1920, and to be put before the Standing Conference on the following day. Muir was unable to attend these meetings but he wrote a savage letter to the Chairman, which he asked should be read to the Conference, criticizing the

new draft which 'instead of frankly recognising the limi-
tations and deficiencies of the Bureau...labours to
suggest that the Bureau is a wholly admirable institution'. Muir admitted, however, that a number of
changes which Hartog had proposed in the draft would
amend the worst defects of the document; and it is
probable that the gentle wisdom of Hartog (who was at
this time Academic Registrar in the University of
London) prevailed at the meeting. In the event, an
amended draft was approved and published[1] and was
circulated in May to member universities, together with
an inquiry as to whether the universities of the Empire
would be in favour of a Royal Charter for the Bureau
in place of its Articles of Association. There were two
reasons for suggesting that the Bureau should have a
Royal Charter: one, that Hartog and others had criticized the Articles of Association in two respects (they
were altered in 1921 to meet these criticisms); and the
other, that the Committee thought a Royal Charter
would be 'more dignified than Articles of Association
under the Companies Acts'. In his circular letter to
vice-chancellors Hill did add that the cost of securing a
Royal Charter might be considerable.

Any decision to seek a Royal Charter would have had
to be made at a general meeting of the whole Congress
in 1921. But the question was settled before then by the
unfavourable response of the universities to Hill's
circular. Of thirty-six replies only nine were in favour
of a Royal Charter, one was neutral and twenty-six were

[1] *Universities Bureau of the British Empire: a Statement of its Aims and
Objects* (50 Russell Square, London, W.C. 1) (no date).

opposed, some of them very strongly so. The Principal of Aberdeen 'deprecated the Bureau or its Committee being endowed with any status which it has not at present'. Queen's, Belfast, was 'entirely opposed to the Bureau going to the expense'. Oxford objected to the proposal and gave warning that if a Charter were applied for, the university would not be advised to contribute to the cost. The matter was therefore dropped, the Articles of Association were amended to meet the criticisms Hartog and others had raised,[1] and the Committee turned its attention to preparations for the 1921 Congress.

Constitutional overhaul

It was nine years before the constitution of the Bureau was considered again. In 1929 Hill died. Frank Heath, who had been Secretary of the Department of Scientific and Industrial Research, was invited to give advice, and subsequently to succeed Hill as full-time Secretary, and a sub-committee was appointed to consider in consultation with Heath 'the whole question of the reorganisation of the work of the Bureau'.[2] Heath found much needing to be done. Costs were rising, and the Bureau was faced with preparations for another Congress in 1931. The staff was too small and was constantly overworked. The lease of 50 Russell Square was running out; the house was not in good condition (the Executive Committee

---

[1] This was agreed at a meeting of the Executive on 18 March 1921.

[2] Executive Committee minutes, 13 July 1929. The sub-committee consisted of T. F. Sibly (Vice-Chancellor of Reading), P. Giles (Master of Emmanuel College, Cambridge), T. Loveday (Vice-Chancellor of Bristol) and E. Deller (Principal of London).

minutes are peppered with reports of cracks in the plaster, subsidence, and settlement of walls); it was not large enough; it was shared with sub-tenants;[1] and the terms for renewing the lease were an increase in rent from £130 to £400 a year. Heath attacked these problems with characteristic vigour. He proposed increases in staff which would double the annual expenditure. He renewed the lease but began negotiations for a new building with much better facilities at 88*a* Gower Street (which the Bureau occupied shortly afterwards). And he prepared a paper embodying fresh Articles of Association, to remedy a number of defects which had become more and more troublesome as the Bureau's responsibilities and prestige had increased. This paper set sail on a smoother sea than did the papers prepared by Hill and Muir ten years earlier. It was accepted by the Executive as a basis for a new constitution, circulated to universities at home and overseas for comment and criticism, and an amended version was ready in time for the 1931 Congress. There, it did run into stormy weather, but after a discussion which went on all day, and with a string of amendments which clearly taxed the patience of the Chairman, a new constitution of the Bureau was approved. It was subsequently adopted by the Bureau Committee and embodied in revised Articles of Association, which were approved by the Board of Trade on 16 October 1931.

---

[1] This at the beginning of the tenancy, while the Bureau secretariat was small, was a great advantage, for there was a nucleus of 'university consulates' among the tenants: the American University Union in Europe (and for a time the Commonwealth Fund of the Harkness Foundation), the Office National des Universités et Ecoles Françaises, and the British Bureau of the Danish Students' International Committee.

What were the changes in constitution advocated by Heath at this time? In the Memorandum of Association, which sets out the functions and purposes of the Bureau, there was no change. The only changes concerned membership, subscriptions, and mode of government. Over membership the original Articles provided for personal membership—'such persons...as shall have subscribed the Memorandum of Association and such other persons as shall...be appointed by...any University...'. The revised Articles restricted membership to corporate bodies—universities and colleges—and excluded individuals as members. Over subscriptions the original Articles stated that members 'shall not be required to pay any entrance fee or subscriptions' (a reasonable provision since the members were persons, not corporate bodies), and the expenses were to be defrayed out of contributions and donations. The revised Articles prescribed minimum subscriptions for membership depending on the location of each university (whether at home or abroad) and its student-numbers. Over mode of government the original Articles provided nothing but an Executive Committee 'appointed from amongst the Members of the Association'; the number to be not less than ten nor more than twenty, with a quorum of three. The Executive Committee had 'full power to carry out the objects of the Association' with an obligation to call a general meeting of the Association at least once a year. The revised Articles replaced the Executive Committee by an Executive Council consisting of twenty-one members chosen from the representatives of Ordinary members as follows:[1] Great Britain and Ireland, nine; Australia and South Africa, two each; Canada and India, three each; New Zealand, and 'other parts of the Empire', one each.

Fortunately we have a verbatim record of the discussion at the 1931 Congress, when the revised Articles were submitted to a business meeting for approval. They had a very difficult passage, and if the meeting had been under less skilled chairmanship than that of Thomas Holland (Principal of Edinburgh) the revisions might have been rejected altogether. The discussion started well and by mid-morning the Articles were adopted 'in principle'. Then came a consideration of amendments, many of which had been circulated beforehand. These were considered—and most of them rejected—before the lunch break. The Chairman opened the afternoon session by reminding the meeting that the Bureau which would be created by the revised Articles would be only 'an instrument that will act as your attorney to carry out any special wishes you may have'; any fear that the Bureau would infringe the autonomy of the universities was groundless, and delegates should not take the discussion so seriously! Nevertheless, James Baillie, who had succeeded Sadler as Vice-Chancellor of Leeds, forthwith plunged into a belligerent criticism of the revised Articles. He suggested that they were possibly illegal, in that they invited corporate bodies to become members of a corporate body (to which Frank Heath

---

[1] Membership was, in the final draft of the new Articles, divided into: Ordinary members (universities); Associate members (universities in Mandated Territories and university colleges or colleges of universities), and Additional members (a general category embracing other institutions of higher education).

35

blandly replied that if there had been any such risk of illegality the legal advisers at the Board of Trade would have spotted it). In any case, Baillie preferred the old system of personal membership to the proposed system of corporate membership, on the grounds that personal members could not commit their universities, whereas a Council representing corporate members would acquire too much power. (Sibly, from Reading, reminded him that the Articles provided for compulsory subscriptions, and that if membership were to be personal and not corporate, either subscriptions would have to be dropped or members would be personally liable to pay them.) Baillie then made a point which he was fond of making at meetings of the Vice-Chancellors' Committee, namely that the governing bodies of all member universities should be consulted before any changes were decided upon (to which Sibly replied that the draft had in fact been circulated long before to all member universities and that no comments had come from Baillie's own university of a kind which would 'challenge the whole principle on which the new Articles are based'). James Irvine, the Principal of St Andrews, supported Baillie and for a time it looked as though the whole reorganization of the Bureau, which was so patently necessary and on which Heath and the Executive had spent so many months, was in jeopardy. But Michael Sadler saved the day. With consummate tact and charm he admitted both the weight of Baillie's criticisms and the force of Sibly's reply, and then proceeded to propose a sentence which would 'secure us against the dangers to which Sir James Baillie has drawn attention and at the same time preserve the machinery which the Committee have framed'. The sentence was: 'Provided that the powers of the Association shall not be exercised in any such way as to restrict the powers and duties exercised by the constituent members under the several charters, statutes, regulations and other instruments of their self-government.' Under this emollient the irritation quickly subsided and, after a little discussion about rates of subscription, the revised Articles were approved. The querulous goddess who presides over university autonomy had been propitiated, and that sufficed to calm the critics. The emended Articles were adopted by the Bureau at an Extraordinary General Meeting held some months later. It was only later still that the full irony of the incident became apparent: the Board of Trade would not permit Sadler's amendment to be included in the Articles of Association: the act of propitiation was not acceptable to the legal draftsman!

For over thirty years, since the stormy meeting at Edinburgh in 1931, the Bureau's constitution has worn well and has required very little patching. There was only one other moment of danger, when the sense of cohesion among Commonwealth universities seemed to weaken. That was in 1946, when the fatigue of war and preoccupation with their domestic post-war problems left universities very little energy to think about inter-university affairs. The proposal that there should be another quinquennial congress in 1948 met with a luke-warm reception among—for instance—some of the universities of Canada. It was the chairman of the British Committee of Vice-Chancellors and Principals

37

(Hector Hetherington) who rekindled enthusiasm. He arranged, with the help of a grant from the Nuffield Foundation, for the heads of Canadian universities to be invited to Britain for a private meeting with British vice-chancellors at Corpus Christi College, Oxford, from 15 to 17 July 1947. Among the topics discussed at this meeting was the future of the Bureau. The meeting was (in the words of one of the heads of universities who attended it) 'a roaring success'. The community of interests between Commonwealth universities was reaffirmed. One of the viable ideas which arose from this meeting was that immediately before (or after) each quinquennial congress the executive heads of Commonwealth universities should meet for a few days; this has been a feature of congresses ever since.

It was not only the cracks and dislocations of war which let a little apathy into the affairs of the Bureau; another cause was that universities outside Britain did not have enough voice in the Bureau's government. Up to 1948 the Executive Council comprised twenty-one members, nine of whom were heads of British universities, and the other twelve were people resident in London with past connexions with overseas universities but no direct responsibility to them. This arrangement was strongly criticized when the Executive heads of all Commonwealth universities met in Bristol before the 1948 Congress in Oxford. As a result of this criticism, the Bureau radically reformed its pattern of government: it confined membership of the Executive Council to heads of universities, from whichever part of the Commonwealth they came (to be represented, when necessary, by proxies personally appointed by Council members); it reduced the number of university seats for the United Kingdom from nine to four; and it arranged for the overseas Executive Council meetings described on p. 56. And so, since 1949, the Bureau's affairs have been run by an Executive Council which has comprised the executive heads of sixteen member universities.[1] Such constitutional changes as have been made have been quietly approved at quinquennial congresses and ratified at subsequent Extraordinary General Meetings. Thus at Oxford in 1948 the obsolete word 'Empire' was, almost silently and with evident relief, dropped and replaced by the word 'Commonwealth'; and at the same time an amendment (in the names of the Principals of McGill and London) was carried which changed 'Bureau' to 'Association': a welcome amendment, for it reminds members that the chief function of the A.U.B.C. is to be a society and not a bureaucracy. Nevertheless (and certainly at the wish of member universities) the activities of the secretariat have increased enormously; this has required periodic increases in subscription, each of which has had to be approved by an Extraordinary General Meeting held during a Congress (the item headed 'subscription rates' always has to be introduced with the utmost tact). The tides of international politics have carried away a few members: universities in Burma and the Irish Republic are not eligible for membership,

[1] Distributed, by decision at the 1948 Congress, as follows: United Kingdom (4), Canada (2), Australia (2), New Zealand (1), South Africa (2), India and Ceylon (2), Pakistan (1), other parts of the Commonwealth (2). Executive heads who reside overseas are empowered to nominate proxies resident in Britain.

and South African universities will relinquish membership at the time of the 1963 Congress; but every year
new members are admitted to the Association.[1]

Throughout all the constitutional changes in the
Articles of Association and the impressive growth of
membership, the purposes and functions of the A.U.B.C.
remain virtually unchanged. The Memorandum of
Association, drawn up hurriedly in 1919 so that the
Bureau could receive £5000 from the Treasury, has not
had to be altered (except for minor verbal amendments
such as those following the obsequies of the word
'Empire'); the purposes set out in that Memorandum
are still the forces of cohesion which bring together over
130 institutions in amicable membership. Indeed the
wording of the memorandum reappears almost intact in
the draft Charter now (1962) before the Privy Council.[2]
And when it became necessary to epitomize its purpose
in a Latin motto, to lie beneath the arms granted to the
Association in 1958, the Association's classical advisers
chose the words: *scientia commune bonum*.[3]

NINE CONGRESSES

The pattern

It is perhaps just as well that pioneers do not realize
the responsibility they carry for creating tradition. The
organizers of the 1912 Congress, feeling their way in a

[1] Appendix III gives figures for membership since 1932.

[2] It is hoped that a Royal Charter will be presented to the Association at its Jubilee Congress in 1963.

[3] The Association's heraldic advisers were less happy in their advice:
the combination of lamp, globe, rose, book and wings doubtless has
appropriate heraldic significance; but to the uninitiated it cannot but
appear as an inelegant sketch for an ill-assorted still-life portrait.

novel venture, set a pattern which—with minor varia-
tions—has been followed ever since: selection, by an
organizing committee, of topics from among those suggested by Commonwealth universities; four or five days
of meetings to discuss prepared papers on these topics;
pre- and post-Congress tours to other universities; a
grand opening, often under royal patronage; a liberal
ration of academic junketing—government receptions,
college dinners, garden parties, and a sprinkling of
honorary degrees—graceful speeches of thanks and
appreciation by overseas delegates; and a business
meeting, to set the Association's compass for another
five years. And so, over the last fifty years the programmes of congresses have fallen into a familiar
routine. As the number of member universities has
increased the congresses have become bigger and (probably a consequence of this) discussions are more formal
and less lively than they were. Since 1948 the executive
heads of universities have had a private meeting of their
own beforehand, where they can concentrate on administrative chores, and where the to and fro of argument is easier. Other noteworthy changes are few and
are easily recorded. In the early days (1921–36) a
handful of students' representatives attended (they must
have found the discussions dull). Since 1921 no congress
has been without its guests from the United States. At
first there were only representatives of bodies such as the
American Council on Education, the Institute of International Education, and the American University
Union; but in 1953 a happy precedent was created by
the decision to invite the Association of American Uni-

versities to nominate ten American university presidents to attend the Congress. This has been a very felicitous innovation: nothing comforts a Commonwealth vice-chancellor more than to realize how much easier his job is than that of an American university president! Until 1958 the congresses were all held in Britain. This was certainly not due to any lack of hospitality on the part of Commonwealth members: indeed R. A. Falconer invited the Congress to meet in Toronto in 1926, and Canada again offered to act as host in 1953; but on each occasion the Association felt obliged to decline the invitations on the grounds that, under the circumstances at the time, it would be harder to assemble a representative gathering of delegates in North America than in Europe. By 1958 these circumstances had changed and the eighth Congress was held in Montreal. It was outstandingly successful and in future every alternate congress will be held in one of the overseas universities of the Commonwealth. The Canadian universities, with generous assistance from the Association of American Universities, organized a number of fabulous post-Congress tours, financed by a grant from the Carnegie Corporation of New York. The educational value of these tours cannot be over-estimated. For scores of the delegates it was a first experience of higher education in Canada and the United States. They saw vividly its immense scale, its vigour, its achievement, and they began to understand its underlying philosophy.

All these congresses seem woven from the same threads of thought. There is a familiarity, not to say monotony, about the problems discussed, but this is surely justified because they are all unsolved problems; it is no indictment of the 1963 Congress that its agenda includes scarcely any topic which has not been part of the fabric of earlier congresses, just as it is no indictment of a clergyman that he continues to preach about sin. And—familiar as the problems are, and as far from solution as ever—it is fascinating to page over congress reports and to listen to the voices of academic giants: Lugard, on the part which a university should play in the training of character; Rutherford and J. J. Thomson, on the training of post-graduates; Sherrington and Jagadis Chandra Bose, on research; Whitehead, on science in general education (an astringent criticism of some ideas we still cherish: 'education', he said dryly, 'is formed out of the accurate accomplishment of a succession of detailed tasks'); Falconer from Toronto, on university finance, and Lord Haldane of Cloan, on pension schemes (which he introduced by way of a comparison between the schools of mathematics in Cambridge and Göttingen). Yet even academic giants cannot have the last word on the unsolved problems which come before successive congresses; as the climate of opinion changes, problems have to be re-examined. Indeed from a study of discussions at earlier congresses it is possible to trace trends in Commonwealth academic opinion over the last fifty years.

Universities and the State

Take the topic of universities and the State. Three times it has been before the Congress: in 1926, in 1948, and in 1953. In 1926 the discussion was led by Lord

43   4·2

Balfour, Chancellor of the Universities of Cambridge and Edinburgh, who said quite bluntly that if the State gave massive financial backing to universities it would be 'a natural and pardonable instinct on the part of the State to control and supervise the working' of universities. Natural and pardonable but, as he went on to say, 'extremely dangerous'. However, the speakers who followed Balfour were reassuring. From various quarters of the Commonwealth came the view that in fact, even in universities heavily subsidized by the State, there were no serious symptoms of State control. Reading between the lines, one gets the impression that the delegates were more concerned about the parsimony of States toward their universities than about the pressures which States might exert on universities. The overtones of the discussion suggest that universities would have liked governments to take more, rather than less, interest in their affairs.

Two decades later it was a different story. By this time the British universities were receiving £10 million annually in grants from the University Grants Committee; the Australian universities, though still seriously under-financed, were beginning to benefit from Federal grants; the Vice-Chancellor of Madras, A. L. Muda-liar, reported that a Central University Grants Commission had just been set up in India. The Chairman of the British University Grants Committee (Walter Moberly) opened the discussion with a masterly description of the policy of his Committee and the ways in which it safeguards itself against any suspicion of control over the universities it finances. Moberly admitted that 'undoubtedly the machinery exists by which the State could, if it were so minded, apply almost irresistible financial pressure to the Universities. The basis of confidence is the conviction not that the State cannot but that the State will not want to do so; it rests, in other words, not upon the law but upon the convention of the Constitution.' It would be true to say that up to 1948 most academics in Britain were satisfied with the strength of this informal and unwritten safeguard; but the delegates in 1948 no longer displayed the easy confidence of their predecessors in 1926. The Vice-Chancellor of Liverpool ventilated, with consummate charm and urbanity, some misgivings even about the operations of the British University Grants Committee. From Canada, from India, from Pakistan, came evidence of slight apprehensions about the consequences of too much reliance on State support without other sources of income, and one of the delegates from South Africa was able to say bluntly—even fourteen years ago—'there is quite definite political interference and also municipal interference with the universities'. The truth of the matter is—and this has been abundantly confirmed by subsequent history—that universities have not yet learnt how to handle their new patron, who is no longer a queen or a prince or a bishop (we have acquired the techniques for handling these dignitaries) but is the taxpayer, the man-in-the-street, speaking through his representative in Parliament. Fresh techniques are needed to bring this new patron closer to the universities he helps to finance. Ivor Jennings, who was then Vice-Chancellor of the University of Ceylon, mentioned one technique for enlisting the understanding of the new patron. It is a simple but important measure which could certainly be commended to universities in other new democracies. There was (Jennings told the Congress) a large measure of autonomy in his university because the Government of Ceylon

has maintained the conventions which it was hoped would be established when the constitution was laid down. One reason is that the Legislature is given adequate representation in the Court of the University.... The presence of elected members of the House of Representatives and the Senate of Ceylon in the Court enables those bodies to have adequate information about University activities.... Therefore, strangely enough, the existence of those representatives in the Court of the University has contributed to University autonomy rather than the reverse.

Five years later, in 1953, the topic was again before the Congress. On this occasion the case in favour of State aid in Britain was presented by the Chancellor of the Exchequer himself, R. A. Butler. By this time practically all Commonwealth universities were reconciled to dependence on government grants. There was evidence, from the President of the University of British Columbia, that universities were learning the only sensible and practical way to deal with their new patrons, namely through 'the education of the public, of legislators and of governments, about the proper functions of the universities, about the contributions which they can and should make to their communities and their governments, and about the importance of freedom to them in respect of this—freedom in the sense that the "authority" or the "expert" must have freedom if he is to function effectively'. This theme, of 'freedom with service', was thrown into contrast with the attitude which prevailed then (it has changed somewhat since) in the United States over Federal aid to universities. President Dodds of Princeton put up a vigorous defence of the private university and told the Congress why massive Federal aid to higher education was in America regarded as particularly unwelcome: 'the exhortation' (he said) 'that Federal aid to private universities must be innocent of any attendant governmental control is an unrealistic piece of wishful thinking'. As they listened to President Dodds, even the most severe critics of the British University Grants Committee and its replicas in other countries must have reflected how comparatively successful we have been in the Commonwealth over educating our legislators in the purposes and privileges of universities; and it is agreeable to recollect that some of this education has been achieved through A.U.B.C. congresses.[1]

Other perennials

'Universities and the State' is by no means the only perennial to appear on Congress agenda. Others include what Charles Snow has now christened the 'two

---

[1] It has to be remembered that the whole pattern of Federal aid to universities in America differs from the patterns in most Commonwealth countries. Publicly supported higher education is a responsibility of the States, not the central government, and some early attempts to give Federal aid were actually vetoed on these grounds. During and after the war Federal aid developed in two ways: (1) as aid to veterans under the Servicemen's Readjustment Act 1944 (as happened also in Australia); and (2) through research contracts let by Federal agencies. It was these which justified President Dodds's fears. By 1950 Federal agencies were spending $150 million a year in American colleges and universities; it is estimated that over 70 % of all research being carried on in these institutions was being financed in this way.

cultures': noble attitudes were struck on this theme in 1912, 1921, 1936 and 1953. Whereas the content of discussions on universities and the State has changed slowly and subtly over fifty years the content of discussions on the two cultures has suffered a veritable revolution. In 1921, during a discussion on 'the balance of studies', the Vice-Chancellor of Oxford (L. R. Farnell) spoke of Hellenism and 'the new crisis which threatens its gradual decay'. At the end of his address he proposed (and there is no indication, at any rate in the recorded discussion, that his proposal alarmed the delegates) that students who took an honours degree in modern languages at Oxford should not be awarded a First Class unless they had taken Greek or Latin together with their modern languages. That was in 1921, within the undergraduate days of men still under sixty. A bare generation later, in 1953, a session at the Cambridge Congress was devoted to a topic with what must surely be the most tendentious title ever on the programme of an academic conference: 'What subject or subjects today are best fitted to fulfil the role played previously in the university curriculum by the classics?' Classicists rallied to the rescue, of course. The Vice-Chancellor of Oxford (Maurice Bowra), mindful perhaps of what his predecessor said at a Congress thirty-two years earlier, called the title of the session a 'vicious or an improper question', to be compared with: 'What person is necessary to fulfil the role previously played, up to today, by your wife?' In a speech which alone justified the organizing committee's choice of title, Maurice Bowra uncompromisingly defended the classics. He would not even be satisfied with the classics in translation: 'translation', he said, 'is as interesting as any crossword puzzle—and about as important'. Notwithstanding this and other spirited defences of the classics, including a moving and thoughtful paper from S. Radhakrishnan (when he reminded the Congress that for Indians the classics include Sanskrit and Pali, Arabic and Persian), the current of opinion at the meeting flowed in the same direction as the tendentious title. It was (as Maurice Bowra described it) like 'attending a very distinguished and very elaborate funeral...with *pompes funèbres première classe* and with many valedictory and obituary orations delivered over the grave'.

Other perennial topics beside these two are postgraduate training, on which there has been an almost continuous debate since the institution of the British Ph.D. in 1919, and the interchange and secondment of staff between Commonwealth universities. It is extraordinary how frequently this last topic is talked about and approved and yet how difficult it is to turn pious resolutions into fruitful action. As long ago as 1903 the proto-Congress (see chapter 1) declared its interest in a 'circulation of teaching staff'. At the 1912 Congress detailed plans and estimates for a secondment scheme with Australia were put forward. In 1921 the scope of the discussions widened: G. MacLean appealed to the delegates to promote interchange of staff (and of students) between Commonwealth countries and the United States, using machinery which had been set up immediately after the First World War. The topic was discussed again in 1926 when it seems, from the very

brief record, that enthusiasm for migration of under-
graduates from one university to another had subsided,
and that difficulties—especially of finance—stood in the
way of any substantial development of secondment
programmes for academic staff. In 1936, at the Association's Extraordinary General Meeting, Carleton Stanley,
at that time President of the Canadian Universities
Conference, moved a resolution that a committee should
be set up 'to inquire into the possibility of effecting the
exchange of members of University Teaching Staffs'.
The resolution was carried unanimously, but the war
has obliterated any work the committee may have
done. In 1948 it was, once more, on the agenda, this
time as a series of propositions drawn up by the executive
heads of the member universities. These propositions
were evidently an attempt to overcome the obstacles
which, notwithstanding the fact that air travel had
brought the furthest parts of the Commonwealth within
a few hours of one another, still stood in the way of
aspirations agreed upon as long ago as 1903. The
proposals covered both permanent and temporary
migration of staff: improved arrangements for dealing
with applicants for vacant posts, superannuation schemes
which are not a bar to interchange among Commonwealth countries, special arrangements to encourage
interchange of young post-graduates, the attachment of
scholars on sabbatical leave to host-universities, and
(most realistic of all) an approach to Foundations for
financial help to assist migration of scholars within the
Commonwealth. The propositions were introduced by
the Principal of Glasgow, Hector Hetherington (the

'doyen of Commonwealth academic meetings', whose eloquent and moving address was the most memorable speech at the eighth Congress in Montreal in 1958). Everyone agreed with them in principle and after an amicable discussion and a few innocuous amendments, they were approved. That was fourteen years ago, and it seems now that at long last the chief obstacles in the way of Commonwealth interchange have been lifted. The Commonwealth University Interchange Scheme, run by the British Council, the Commonwealth Scholarship and Fellowship Plan, the grants given by Foundations, the activities of the British Department of Technical Co-operation under Andrew Cohen: all these have smoothed the path from one university to another. If there is a problem remaining for discussion it is the balance of direction in traffic: the current bringing overseas academics to Britain is all too strong compared with the current carrying British academics to India or Australia or Nigeria. It is a pity that an outmoded insularity makes the British still so unappreciative of the attractions for scholars in parts of the Commonwealth outside their own island; so unappreciative that opportunities for travel away from Europe often go begging. Perhaps there is something lacking in the public relations of Commonwealth universities; otherwise the British scholar would surely be more excited about India and Pakistan as centres for Oriental studies, tropical Africa for the earth sciences and social anthropology, not to mention the older Dominions for the sake of individual scholars who have built up vigorous schools of research there. This question of the balance of traffic, touched upon by the Vice-Chancellor of McGill as long ago as 1903, may perhaps appear on the agenda of some future Congress. It ought to.

Some neglected topics

Let us take one more glance at the eight volumes of congress Reports. A few topics have fallen out of fashion, a few have come into fashion, and there are some topics, vividly important within universities, which somehow have failed to find their way into congress programmes. Among the topics which have now become unfashionable are adult education, not discussed since 1921; the training of teachers, discussed only twice, in 1921 and 1936; physical education in universities, discussed in 1926 and 1936; and university finance, discussed in 1921, but since then (and this is significant) subsumed under university–government relations. Among the newcomers to congress programmes (and this, too, is significant) are the admission and selection of students, which did not appear at a congress meeting until 1953;[1] and a discussion of new universities, held in 1958. Three important subjects which have received surprisingly little attention are examinations, discussed only in 1936; the moral and ethical implications of university work (discussed only in 1912 and, obliquely, in 1948, and productive of some of the most penetrating fragments of thinking to appear at congresses); and,

[1] The story is told of one Cambridge college that when a new Senior Tutor was appointed in the 1920's he asked the Master what College policy was over admissions. The Master's reply was: 'Policy! We have 66 beds in the College. If you have 60 of them filled by October 1st you'll be doing well.' This same college now has some 800 applications for about 100 places each year.

most surprising of all, university government and administration. This last topic appeared on the agenda of the first Congress, under a title still of vital interest to university teachers, namely the 'Representation of Teachers and Graduates on the Governing Body of a University'. The topic did not reappear for forty-one years, and then under a different guise: the competing claims of administrative and academic duties (when Lawrence Bragg made the melancholy calculation that in the average civic university some £90,000 a year of academic staff's time is spent on committee work!). In 1958 it appeared again, this time disguised under the question: 'Who should determine university policy?', when the Chancellor of Chicago University in a sparkling speech described the functions of an American university president as 'midwife to the faculty', adding that the successful president, like the successful obstetrician, delivers the product and then intentionally steps into the background. There must have been more than one Commonwealth vice-chancellor present who wondered wistfully whether he, too, qualified for this description. It was a surprising feature of this discussion that so much attention was given to the part administrators play in policy-making, and so little attention was given to the specific topic discussed in 1912, namely the representation of university teachers on the bodies where power resides in a modern university. Finally there is the surprising omission repaired only in the Jubilee year of congresses: the place of the layman in university government. Delegations to congresses have always included laymen: chancellors, chairmen of council, honorary treasurers and the like. At eight congresses over fifty years they have sat patiently through discussions of abstruse academic matters, silent (most of them, at any rate—there have been notable exceptions), hearing a great deal about universities as professors see them, but never hearing any talk about a subject which must often have puzzled them, namely what part they as laymen are expected to play in university government. In nearly all universities of the Commonwealth sovereignty resides in a predominantly lay governing body. All the devices of academic propaganda are used to persuade the lay governors that they must on no account *govern*: to do so might constitute an infringement of academic freedom. They take it very well. They accept the taboo as a condition of membership of these strange but impressive societies. They are of immense help to universities: their wisdom, experience and (to put it on its lowest level) their contacts with industry and commerce and government have done much to give the universities their magisterial position in contemporary Britain, a position universities have not occupied since the Middle Ages. But until 1963 they had never been invited to put their point of view to a Congress of the Association of Universities of the British Commonwealth.

One more word before we put these eight volumes back on the shelf. They run to about a million words. They should contain the quintessence of fifty years of academic wisdom. Do they? A little anthology of first-rate writing and thinking could be picked out of them, and another anthology of gracious speeches of welcome and introduction and thanks—the kind of speeches which Lawrence A. Kimpton of Chicago described as short, true, and adding absolutely nothing to the general fund of knowledge. There are some nice snippets of academic wit, including in 1936 a well-deserved riposte from the United States. The riposte arose from a delicate innuendo thrown out by the President of the Board of Education (Oliver Stanley) that although 'a certain foreign university has a Chair for ice-cream making', he hoped nothing of the sort would happen here. To which the representative of the American University Union in London very properly replied (in a discussion of the importance of dietetics in curricula for physical education) that if the foreign country Stanley referred to was America, courses in ice-cream making were probably part of a curriculum on dietetics. 'Unhappily' he went on, 'the President of the Board of Education chose to be oblivious of the Chair of Brewing in a certain well-known University in England [Birmingham]. At all events, in America they find that they make better ice-cream than England makes beer.'

Much of the material in these volumes is not from prepared manuscript but is a transcription of spontaneous discussion: a sort of donnish Hansard. It is a reassuring exercise to put it alongside a political Hansard. Compared with politicians these delegates from Commonwealth universities may have their shortcomings; they may over-simplify issues; they may be over-subtle in argument; they may be tortuous in action: but at least they talk better, incomparably better.

Community of Universities

During the 1948 Congress there was a discussion on inter-university relations. The thoughts of delegates naturally turned to ways in which universities of the Commonwealth could become more familiar with one another, and it was proposed, and agreed, that in the years between congresses there should be smaller meetings in parts of the Commonwealth outside Britain. These smaller occasions took the form of meetings of the Executive Council (although this is not the form in which the original proposal was made). It was a good idea, for at Executive Council meetings in London all but the British universities were represented not by their nominees but by proxies. And it was an idea which has proved outstandingly valuable, not so much because of the business which has been transacted but because it has enabled universities all over the Commonwealth to be at home to their colleagues from elsewhere in the Commonwealth, and more than any other activity of the Association this has cemented the universities of the English-speaking world into one family. From 1949 to 1956 these overseas meetings were financed by the generosity of the Nuffield Foundation. A list of the conferences held between congresses is given in Appendix VI. No record of the business transacted or the itineraries completed can do justice to the deep impression made by these visitations. They have served as workshops of Commonwealth understanding and sympathy. A brief eye-witness account of the third of these—a visit fifteen academics paid to India in 1951—must suffice.

The invitation came from the Inter-University Board of India. The delegates comprised representatives from Australia, Canada, Hong Kong, New Zealand, Pakistan, South Africa, the United Kingdom and West Africa. The Conference was opened in Delhi by the President of India on 21 December 1951, and it closed with a session in Bombay on 16 January 1952. Between these two days of formal meetings there was a marathon of sightseeing, the like of which the delegates had never experienced before and probably never will again. The Indian government and the universities provided hospitality that was both generous and considerate: considerate because they reduced speeches and conferences in senate rooms to a minimum, and instead gave the delegates a vivid impression of the rich cultural heritage of India and opportunities to talk with students, scholars and leaders in political life. On every side there was evidence of Indian goodwill toward other countries in the Commonwealth, and readiness on the part of Indians to discuss their own problems frankly and objectively.

The delegates were given a chartered plane for their tour. Their almost daily experience was to land (usually an hour or more late, but this was not the fault of the chartered plane) at an airport, to receive the greetings from a patient reception committee, and to undergo a bewilderment of fresh (and often fantastic) experiences: they were pursued by a snake charmer in Agra, they rode four at a time on State elephants in Jaipur, they were adorned with garlands of flowers in Nagpur, and two of the delegates, contrary to their inclinations, were induced to sing 'Waltzing Matilda' before a select audience in the State theatre at Mysore, in the presence of His Highness the Maharajah.

The Conference itself was little more than a minor incident in the delegation's tour. There was a session on the 'Role of universities in the promotion of Social Welfare' in which fifteen speakers took part; although (as some of them confessed) all that was to be said on the subject had been said by the first five of them. It was interesting to hear some of the speakers declare that universities should intervene in public affairs and even offer judgement on controversial social and political issues; though our impression was that these were minority and not majority views among Indian educationists. The Executive in Madras discussed (without reaching any very clear conclusion) some of the problems of interchange of staff and students, particularly between Commonwealth countries outside Great Britain. There was a general approval of the proposed arrangements for the 1953 Congress and the Executive were satisfied to leave the detailed arrangements to the Secretary, in consultation with the officers of the Association in the United Kingdom. When the Secretary sought guidance on the policy he should adopt for the *Universities Yearbook*, he received assurances that the Executive were happy about his present policy and were content that he should pursue it at his own discretion.

The formal meeting was a good opportunity for an exchange of views among delegates. But the main purpose of the tour was accomplished informally. In conversations over meals and while walking through colleges, in visits to old palaces and temples and tombs, in witnessing India's first elections by universal suffrage (which took place while the delegates were there), a handful of Commonwealth university men received an indelible impression of the greatness of India's history and culture, the immensity of her present problems in dispelling illiteracy and improving higher education, and her quiet determination to tackle these problems and to solve them by democratic means.

This is a typical experience of one of the inter-congress meetings. How abundantly it justifies the tentative suggestions made by Hector Hetherington after an informal conference of British and Canadian universities in 1947! Discussing the outcome of this conference, he said:

...we need more frequent contact on the executive level than is provided by the quinquennial conferences. Vice-Chancellors, Presidents, Deans, etc., are, of course, only means to ends. But they are the only or at least the best means to certain ends. There is something to be said in favour of at least small representative meetings like this [the Anglo-Canadian one just concluded] every year, in different parts of the Empire.

One other recent innovation deserves a place in this chapter, namely the very informal joint conferences, arranged by the Association's secretariat, and attended by a number of British vice-chancellors and a team of American university presidents nominated by the Association of American Universities. The first of these was held in Birmingham in 1956, the second in Cambridge in 1961, and the third in New York in 1962. It has now been decided to continue the meetings, one in each inter-congress period, alternately in Britain and the United States. Skeleton programmes are prepared to hold the conferences together, but their real purpose is to enable the heads of American and British universities to exchange views privately, uninhibited by secretaries taking notes and undeterred by the fear that they might be quoted afterwards. To watch Americans politely accepting sherry—the Cambridge tribal drink—and making the best of the sad fact that it is not Bourbon; and to hear a fresh crop of academic jokes harvested over dinner, may give a false impression of these meetings. They are in fact of the greatest significance. Here is one example. The United States is now deeply involved in exporting higher education to tropical Africa: for a day or more at the Cambridge meeting in 1961 there was an earnest discussion of this topic. There is no doubt at all that this discussion is leading to more fruitful Anglo-American co-operation over higher education in Africa.

CHAPTER III

THE VICE-CHANCELLORS' COMMITTEE

ORIGINS

W. M. Childs's memorandum

This is not the place for a full history of the Committee of Vice-Chancellors and Principals of the Universities of the United Kingdom; yet no portrait of the Association would be complete without a sketch of this Committee, for it is in a sense the eldest child of the old Bureau of Universities of the Empire and its affairs still remain one of the major responsibilities of the secretariat.

The story of the Committee's birth, in a room in the Foreign Office on 9 May 1918, has already been told. But even committees are not born without a period of gestation, and it is impossible to interpret the momentous decision made in May 1918 without knowing something of the maturation of ideas which preceded it. Fortunately we have some record of this maturation. It began as long ago as 1887 with the occasional *ad hoc* meetings described in the opening paragraphs of this book. The meetings were solely to take counsel on questions arising out of university grants. Their status was vague and informal. If questions other than Treasury grants were raised the outcome was seldom effective because some of those attending the meetings did not feel themselves at liberty to concur in decisions proposed in regard to such questions. The meetings were migratory: now at one college and now at another. They had no organization: no chairman and no secretary, and no particular person responsible for convening them.

On 29 April 1911, at one of these meetings of academic heads, the Principal of University College, Reading (W. M. Childs), proposed that the universities and university colleges of England and Wales should devise some more effective machinery for joint action. He subsequently embodied his proposals in a memorandum (dated 20 January 1912) in which he proposed a 'Central Council of the modern universities and university colleges of England and Wales'. It was a shrewd and prescient and realistic memorandum which deserves to be preserved. Childs urged that some means of effective common action would soon become necessary:

The 'go-as-you-please' stage in the creation and development of University centres is ended or ending. Numerous considerations point to an epoch of direction and organisation, claiming to be judicious and necessary, which may or may not express itself in avowed regulation or control but certainly will express itself, and is now expressing itself, in pressure. There is no need to elaborate the argument. It will be sufficient to call to mind these points:

(*a*) The immense extension of Board of Education power over the whole field of education in the last ten or fifteen years. It is superfluous to illustrate this, but it may be mentioned that some Universities have suffered sharply from the recent incursion of the Board into the field of agricultural education.

(*b*) The disposition, visible enough in politics, to extend the sphere of State responsibility.

(*c*) The attitude of the Labour party to University

questions—an attitude possibly not unfriendly to Universities, but certainly not an attitude of untempered acquiescence in things as they are, nor averse to the method of interference.

(*d*) The transference of the control and administration of the Treasury Grants from the Treasury to the Board of Education.[1] In this connexion it should be noted that the Board now appears in the preface to the University Blue-Book as answerable to the public for the new Universities and Colleges, that the 'Statement of Grants' issued last summer carried with it not only alleged advantages but a considerable extension of the Board's supervision and discretion, and that the interview between the Academic Heads and the new Advisory Committee which took place on 18 October demonstrated that the new Committee intend to take their function more seriously than the previous Advisory Committee of the Treasury. While it would be unreasonable to quarrel with the Committee's attitude in this respect, or to doubt the sincerity of individual members who have used strong expressions about freedom, it should be borne in mind that vigilance and efficiency on the part of a Committee entrusted with this function can hardly express itself otherwise than through advice weighted by financial rewards and penalties. What is to be apprehended in the general situation is not the issue of drastic regulations affecting Universities, nor acts of arbitrary interference, so much as an increase, little by little, and step by step, of advisory and supervisory pressure, justified in the public mind by excellent reasons, difficult to resist, but in the long run more prejudicial to freedom and spontaneity than provocative intervention.

(*e*) The recently published Report of the Consultative Committee, on Secondary School Examinations, is a striking

---

[1] From 1887, when the first State grants in modern form were made to universities, the grants were administered by a Committee of the Treasury. In 1910 administration of university grants was transferred to the Board of Education. In 1918 it reverted to the Treasury, where it still is.

reminder of the way in which questions of profound interest and importance to Universities may at any time enter the stage of public discussion which is the prelude to some kind of settlement. It appears to some readers at least that the Universities do not play a very effective part in the settlement proposed in the Report, and it seems reasonable to submit that here is a question upon which it is most desirable on many grounds that their authoritative opinion should be heard.

(*f*) Lastly, the State already gives to the new Universities and Colleges more than twenty-five per cent of their collective revenue. This proportion will increase, and in the absence of a public opinion not yet educated to understand that the best way of getting service from Universities is to give them money and leave them free, the consequences are too obvious to need mention here.

It is submitted that, in the absence of more effective means of joint action by Universities than at present exist, the perils suggested by these considerations are real. Indeed, we know them to be so from experience. The forces tending in the direction of avowed or veiled control by the State over Universities and their policy, in common with every other branch of education, cannot be disarmed or checked by ignoring or belittling them, or by leaving individual Universities to fight their own battles, or by trusting that when common action is at last made necessary by a great emergency it will prove invincible. It is submitted that two things are requisite: (1) the closer union of Universities and Colleges, and the growth of a habit of taking counsel and action together; and (2) the assertion by Universities and Colleges of the importance of preserving as an active principle not only for themselves, but for every branch of national education, another idea—the idea and fact of liberty, individuality, local initiative, spontaneity and variety. The increasing pressure of central authority, the very success of the continued movement to reorganize all our education in accordance with standards imposed by or urged from the centre makes it necessary as never before to emphasize these vital things. That should be the work of the new Universities and Colleges.[1]

There was no lack of material of common interest to the universities. Already the newer universities had a common interest in the allocation of Treasury grants and the policy toward them of what was at that time a Board of Education Committee; in the conditions attaching to subsidies from the Ministry of Agriculture to universities and colleges with agricultural departments; in the regulations for the training of teachers; and in the examination system in secondary schools.

Childs proposed a Council with four representatives from each institution, a permanent chairman, and a secretariat. He excluded the universities of Oxford and Cambridge, which at that time were not receiving any Treasury grant, and the Scottish and Irish universities, on the grounds that their inclusion would make concerted action more difficult. His proposition did not meet with the immediate approval of the *ad hoc* committee of academic heads at their 1912 meeting. Then the war came; the problems of universities were shelved; and it was not until 1918, under the ægis of the Bureau, that a Committee was created with the functions Childs had in mind. In its early days it was a very tentative and hesitant body, reluctant to commit itself and desperately

[1] Proposals by the Principal of University College, Reading, for making more effective the existing means of joint action by the new Universities and University Colleges. A private document dated 20 January 1912 and signed 'W. M. C.', circulated to the Vice-Chancellors and Principals of the new English and Welsh universities and university colleges.

anxious not to commit its constituent universities. It met four times a year (it now meets monthly). Upon the creation of this Committee, the *ad hoc* business conferences of universities (the so-called Standing Conference which formally created the Committee of Vice-Chancellors and Principals) lapsed and were replaced, from 1922 on, by more formal Conferences of the Home Universities where papers were read and discussed and abstracts of proceedings published.[1]

University finance

The first Chairman of the Committee was the Principal of Glasgow, Donald MacAlister, who has already played a leading part in this story. He was a great figure in academic politics, who reigned over the Committee until his retirement in 1929. He and his colleagues found themselves faced with formidable problems. Arrangements for the new Ph.D. degree went satisfactorily (Birmingham and Cambridge were the first two universities to establish the degree); and good progress was made in attracting post-graduates from overseas to come to Britain (by 1924 there were thirty Americans, sixty-two Indians, and sixteen Australians and New Zealanders in London University working for Ph.D.'s). The really difficult problem was finance. On 22 November 1918,

[1] Thus in 1922 three or four representatives from each of the twenty-two universities and university colleges in the Kingdom met in University College, London, to discuss papers on the need for enlarged opportunities for advanced study and research, the need for more residential accommodation, the desirability that certain universities should specialize in certain subjects, and on adult education as an integral part of university work: all topics which are still part of the meagre repertoire for Home Universities Conferences.

the Committee briefed a deputation, which was to wait the next day upon the Chancellor of the Exchequer, the President of the Board of Education, the Secretary for Scotland, and the Chief Secretary for Ireland. The universities had received a circular (written by Fisher, the President of the Board of Education) asking three questions: Is the present system and scale of annual grants satisfactory? How far is it necessary to supplement annual grants by grants toward capital expenditure on buildings and equipment? How far are existing conditions satisfactory as to fees payable by university students?

The Committee expressed itself as satisfied with the system of allocating grants (a tribute to the activities of the newly formed University Grants Committee under McCormick), but emphatically not with the scale of grant. For the universities had to cope with a flood of ex-service students; they had to recover from the inevitable neglect of their fabric during the war; and they had to fit themselves for a massive development of scientific research; and to do all these things under conditions of inflation. The government did what it could to help, but by 1920 the Committee determined to send another deputation to the Chancellor to emphasize the financial embarrassment of the universities. This was forestalled by an announcement in the House of Lords (by Lord Crawford) that the Chancellor would increase the recurrent grant by £500,000. A year later the so-called 'Geddes Axe' fell: the Chancellor (Auckland Geddes) had to make drastic cuts in government expenditure and he proposed to cut the University vote by

£300,000.[1] The Committee protested, but in vain. The cut had to be endured. In November 1924 another deputation (comprising one representative from each university together with representatives of the Association of University Teachers) waited on the government, this time successfully. The Chancellor (Winston Churchill) promptly added £300,000 to the amount available for distribution to the universities (a total of £1·55 million); and the grant was maintained at this level for the whole of the quinquennium 1925–30.

So much for government grants. Although they have been a preoccupation of the Committee ever since, they have been a potent force of cohesion among universities. Whatever other divergences of view there might be among universities, they all concurred in wanting more money from the Treasury. Another matter of common concern was fees. In this matter the universities did not find themselves in agreement. The Committee rejected a proposal that fees in corresponding faculties in all British universities should be uniform. This was a very reasonable disagreement: in Scotland (for example) a reduction in fees at that time would simply have relieved the finances of the Carnegie Trust; whereas in Wales the university had been offered the proceeds of a penny rate provided half the sum received was devoted to the abolition of fees. The Committee soon became flexible enough to accept such disagreements without anxiety.

[1] The effective cut on British universities was £220,000. The other £80,000 was saved by reason of the withdrawal of Treasury support from the Irish universities on the occasion of the treaty with Southern Ireland and the establishment of independent government in Northern Ireland.

Before reaching any conclusion on a matter of such domestic interest to each university the Committee adopted the policy it has followed ever since, namely to consult each university governing body and to circulate among its members the consolidated replies.[1]

Other topics (some of them still on the agenda of the Committee) which the vice-chancellors and principals discussed in the 1920's include the equivalence of degrees and diplomas from foreign universities as qualifications for study in British universities; discussion (at which a representative of the Colonial Office attended) of openings in the Colonial Service for graduates; whether the Burnham Scale for teachers should recognize a second class honours degree as a 'good honours degree' for purposes of salary; limitation of numbers of students admitted to certain faculties; the desirability of having a common entrance requirement among British universities (a hardy perennial still on the agenda paper); advice over the establishment of the Commonwealth Fund Fellowships (now known as the Harkness Fellowships); participation in a National Committee for Intellectual Co-operation (one of those vapid and pretentious bodies which British academics profoundly distrust and which have to be set up for political reasons); and whether there could be agreed common salary scales for academic staff in the various universities.

[1] This is still the general principle on which the Committee operates, though in fact over fees the recent practice has been for a subcommittee to make recommendations without first seeking the views of universities.

Slowly the Committee consolidated itself into a useful consultative body. From the outset it had no official status and no authority to commit the universities, and it still has none. It is a point of cohesion for university policy in Britain: nothing more. Nevertheless, for a time it was under suspicion from one or two universities. In 1929, for example, the Committee agreed on a draft memorandum to be sent to the Chancellor of the Exchequer about university grants; but this concurrence of opinion was challenged by the Vice-Chancellor of Leeds University (the same J. B. Baillie who took such a vigorous part in discussion of the Bureau's constitution in 1931) whose University took the view that any document submitted on behalf of universities to the Chancellor of the Exchequer should be agreed by the governing bodies of all the universities. The Committee disregarded this challenge and sent the memorandum to the Treasury, whereupon the Registrar of Leeds University wrote to the Committee to say: 'The University Council deplores the action of the Committee in sending the memorandum without first securing the sanction of the governing bodies of the universities...and regards the procedure...as wholly irregular and without precedent.'

This incident is noteworthy because it is about the last sign of any lack of confidence in the Committee to come from its constituent universities. It coincided with an examination, by a sub-committee, of the constitutional position of the Committee and its reconstitution on a more regular basis. For its constitution was indeed irregular. It had been set up by resolution of an *ad hoc* Standing Conference of universities in 1918. It was supposed to report from time to time to this Standing Conference; but the Standing Conference had long ago lapsed; and no subsequent conference of universities had prolonged the Committee's life. The Committee therefore decided to go back to the universities for renewed authority for its existence. It resolved on 1 February 1930, that 'it is desirable in the common interests of the universities of the United Kingdom to constitute a Committee of Vice-Chancellors and Principals for purposes of mutual consultation'. The universities agreed. The Committee was reconstituted and has remained in being in this form (with minor alterations) ever since; and so the prescient act of A. J. Balfour has been preserved. With increasing State interest in universities and increasing scale of financial support from Parliament, the importance of the Committee has enormously increased. It still remains informal and without authority to commit the universities to any decision, however trivial. It is still meticulously careful to give no impression of committing them. It concerns itself with administrative means more than with academic ends. It acts by creating a climate of opinion which profoundly influences policy both among universities and among government departments.

All the time, through the pervasive influence of the Committee, the British universities were brought closer together, and the areas increased in which they found themselves able to take common action. The greater their cohesion the more influence they were able to exert with government departments. When the shadow of another war fell across Europe this cohesion became vitally important. For the universities had to negotiate continually with government departments over evacuation, call-up, essential scientific work, the requisitioning of property and a dozen other topics. During this critical and trying period the Committee achieved what never could have been achieved without a committee: it enabled the universities to act as one consolidated body without prejudice to the traditional differences between them and without infringement of their autonomy. Time has only confirmed the editorial opinion of the scientific journal *Nature*, written when the Committee was only four years old:[1]

The setting up in 1918 of the Standing Committee of Vice-Chancellors and Principals was one of the noteworthy events in the long history of the universities of the United Kingdom. Up to that date each university had been a law unto itself, formulating its own policy and drafting its own ordinances with little regard for the needs or doings of others, save in a few matters which could only be handled by the universities collectively, such, for example, as an appeal to the Chancellor of the Exchequer or the institution of the Ph.D. degree.

IMAGE AND INFLUENCE

The Committee today is as informal and as devoid of power as ever it was. But its influence is very great indeed. It rarely makes pronouncements, but the pronouncements it does make carry great weight. Far from infringing university autonomy the Committee is a

[1] 9 December 1922, p. 747.

powerful instrument for preserving it. An early example of this was in 1931, at the time of the depression, when salary cuts were in the air. The Education Committee of the West Riding of Yorkshire had informed the University of Sheffield that it would continue its grant to the University subject to the University making salary cuts. This was reported to the Committee which resolved (on 31 October 1931) as follows:

The Committee of Vice-Chancellors and Principals recognise that the Universities should, in a time of national emergency, take their due share in necessary economies. They are, however, unanimously of the opinion that while Local Authorities or other external bodies have the right and duty to reduce their grants so far as the discharge of their own responsibilities renders it necessary, any requirement by an authority external to a University that economies in the University should be effected in any particular way, would constitute a grave interference with the autonomy of the University and seriously prejudice its interest and standing among the other Universities of the country.

Cumbersome, perhaps; but an unambiguous sign that the universities of the United Kingdom were becoming fused into a coherent society. Fortunately it is very rarely that the Committee has to take such a line as this; but the strength and mutual loyalty is there, and its very defensive strength is a sure base from which the Committee can conduct its normal and much less militant activities. Strength and mutual loyalty have become very necessary, particularly in the intricate negotiations over academic salaries. Here British vice-chancellors find themselves in an extremely delicate and embarrassing position. The Association of University Teachers in Britain has, very properly, pressed for salary revisions from time to time. But whom are they to press? The vice-chancellors are not employers; they are colleagues. Although the Treasury, advised by the University Grants Committee, is the ultimate paymaster for the bulk of the salary bill, it is emphatically not the employer either. The vice-chancellors could not stand by silently while a body resembling a trade union negotiates, with a government department, salary revisions for universities which are independent corporations. Nor would it be feasible for the vice-chancellors to negotiate on behalf of university teachers, for they might not always find themselves in agreement with the proposals their teaching colleagues put up. And so over the last two decades of inflation a great deal of the Committee's time is spent in tortuous discussions over the tactics of salary revision, in circumstances where each of the three negotiating bodies has direct access to the other two. Here, too, the Committee has earned respect from both sides, though it has not been immune from criticism.

It is in keeping with its passion for circumspection that the Committee very rarely makes public statements, though it has of late showed signs of overcoming its modesty in this respect. Its first excursion into publicity was the issue, in July 1946, of *A Note on University Policy and Finance in the Decennium 1947–56*.[1] The note was

---

[1] A sixteen-page pamphlet printed for the Committee and issued on 6 July 1946. It is the first-fruit of a decision made earlier in the year that the Committee 'could advantageously exercise a much greater measure of initiative than hitherto in preparing and in presenting to the Universities, the University Grants Committee and to other bodies, studies and recommendations on matters of common University interest and policy'.

74

prompted by the release, into the invigorating post-war atmosphere, of a flock of buoyant government reports which directly affected the universities: Goodenough on medical education, Loveday on veterinary education, McNair on teacher-training, Percy on technical education, Teviot on dental education; finally the Barlow Report on that wretched abstraction, 'scientific man-power', which recommended the doubling of the number of graduates in science over the pre-war number. The purpose of the note from the Vice-Chancellors' Committee was to put in front of the government and the public the massive developments necessary in universities if they were to fulfil Britain's post-war needs. It is a fascinating document for an understanding of the Committee's growing self-confidence and prestige. True enough, the note begins with a warning that its opinions 'are not to be taken as necessarily those of any university, since the memorandum has not undergone scrutiny by any body other than the Committee of Vice-Chancellors and Principals, by whose authority it is issued'. But a page or two later the note has shed any residual diffidence and has become reassuringly clear-cut and magisterial: '...in no single University ought a great increase in one major Faculty to be unaccompanied by increases to match it in other major Faculties...if the University population must be doubled in science, it must be doubled all round.' And by the time the Report reached page fourteen, the Vice-Chancellors were virtually committing themselves to what was, surely, a revolution in the relationship between universities and the State.

6-2

Community of Universities

There are matters, some of them mentioned in Part I, which visibly touch the welfare and organisation of the Universities, but which are incapable of decision without guidance from Government, since Government alone has the information on which a prudent judgment may be based. Moreover, the Universities entirely accept the view that the Government has not only the right but the duty to satisfy itself that every field of study which in the national interest ought to be cultivated in Great Britain is in fact being adequately cultivated in the University system and that the resources which are placed at the disposal of the Universities are being used with full regard both to efficiency and to economy.

In the view of the Vice-Chancellors, therefore, the Universities may properly be expected not only individually to make proper use of the resources entrusted to them, but collectively, to devise and execute policies calculated to serve the national interest. And in that task, both individually and collectively, they will be glad to have a greater measure of guidance from Government than until quite recent days they have been accustomed to receive. The main question is as to the form in which that guidance and supervision should be exercised.

Shortly after the issue of this note, the Committee published the Report of a Commission it had set up, under Keith Murray (who has since become Chairman of the University Grants Committee) on Halls of Residence.[1] This, too, committed the Vice-Chancellors (and indeed the universities of Britain) not only to some important and very valuable details about the physical amenities which halls of residence should afford but also to a philosophy of higher education—the necessity of keeping the student on the campus—which is now an article of faith among the British universities.

[1] K. Murray (Chairman), *The Planning of University Halls of Residence* (Oxford, 1948).

76

Three other examples of public pronouncements from the Committee of Vice-Chancellors and Principals will suffice to illustrate the great confidence which the Committee now enjoys among its member universities. The first is a survey, undertaken on behalf of the Committee by R. K. Kelsall to determine, for all students entering in the autumn of 1955, exactly how many candidates there were for places in the universities of Britain, and to how many universities each candidate applied.[1] It was an effective response to the criticism very properly being made against British universities, that at a time of great competition for places, multiple applications from candidates, and ambitious plans for university expansion, there were no adequate data on which to form reliable judgements. The Kelsall Report, though it was relevant only to one particular year, has convinced even the most obstinate opponents of statistics that universities, no less than industries, stand to benefit by collecting facts about their place in society.

The other two public pronouncements illustrate how far the Vice-Chancellors' Committee has travelled from the querulous caution of their deliberations in the 1920's. Both tackle courageously problems which have bedevilled British higher education since the last war. Both concern matters on which the universities are jealous of their autonomy. One seeks to achieve 'alignment of form and approximation in substance' of the present entrance requirements prescribed by different universities. Naturally every university wishes to pre-

[1] R. K. Kelsall, *Applications for Admission to Universities* (A.U.B.C., London, 1957).

serve its right to determine its entrance requirements, and it is in the public interest that there should be some variety of entrance requirements to match the variety of attainments among candidates and to encourage diversity in the curricula of schools. But if a candidate has to seek entrance to five universities in the hope of getting a place in one of them, it is intolerable that his school should have to prepare him for widely differing entrance examinations. It is to minimize this sort of inconvenience that the Vice-Chancellors set up a sub-committee on entrance requirements. The sub-committee's proposals do not infringe the right of universities (or, as is really the case, faculties or departments within universities) to demand reasonable prerequisites in the subjects they require candidates to have studied at school. It remains to be seen how far universities will acquiesce in these proposals, or in the sub-committee's more far-reaching proposals for a 'new pattern' of entrance requirements.[1]

The other recent result of work sponsored by the Vice-Chancellors' Committee is the most dramatic of all.[2] It is the recommendation, which received very cordial acceptance by most universities, to set up a central office to receive applications from candidates for any university (excluding—inevitably—Oxford and Cambridge).[3] This office, now established under the

[1] *Report of a Sub-committee on University Entrance Requirements in England and Wales* (A.U.B.C., London, 1962).

[2] An *ad hoc* Committee on Procedure for Admission of Students: *Report* (1958), *Second Report* (1960) and *Third Report* (1961) (A.U.B.C., London).

[3] Over all sorts of issues, from salary scales to admission requirements, these two universities are reluctant to fit themselves into a national

guidance of the Universities' Central Council on Admissions, circulates the applications to universities in the candidate's order of choice. It is a masterly plan, for it still ensures personal negotiations between universities and the candidates who wish to come to them; at the same time it saves schools a monstrous multiplication of entry forms and referees' letters and it saves universities the embarrassment of considering applicants who may already have been accepted elsewhere.

If there had been no Committee of Vice-Chancellors and Principals, or if the Committee had not in the last forty years earned the confidence of universities and created for itself an impressive public image, these recent acts of leadership on the part of the Committee would not have been possible. Yet they are acts which have become essential for the welfare of British higher education; if the universities themselves had been unable to achieve them, the State would without doubt have had to undertake them.[1] So the idea, sown in the

pattern of higher education. In this particular matter, however, it is not easy for them to co-operate; for freshmen at Oxford or Cambridge commonly come into residence fourteen months after A-level results are published, whereas freshmen at other universities commonly come into residence only two months after A-level results are published. For most candidates, therefore, the machine set up by the Vice-Chancellors' Committee works a year before Oxford and Cambridge could use it.

[1] The Committee's record of leadership is not entirely unblemished; there have been occasions when the Committee—undoubtedly in all sincerity—dragged its collective feet. Over the concept and foundation of the University at Keele, for instance, the Committee's comments were unwisely discouraging (an attitude for which ample amends have since been made); and, over the question whether the new Colleges of Advanced Technology should give degrees and not diplomas, the Committee was until recently less than generous. Its resistance to degrees (the Vice-Chancellors saw the strongest objections to using the title and letters of a Bachelor's degree on the grounds that the words 'B.Tech.' would bestow a label which would not mean what the public

academic mind through Childs's prophetic memorandum in 1912, and nurtured by A. J. Balfour's speech at the Foreign Office in 1918, has grown into something of incalculable importance for British universities. It is agreeable to remember, on the occasion of the Association's Jubilee, that the British Committee of Vice-Chancellors and Principals is in a sense a child of the Association of Universities of the Commonwealth and that this Commonwealth-wide society continues to supply a secretariat for the Committee.

is led to expect it to mean, and would therefore imply something which would not be true) was—to put it mildly—disingenuous. Here again the Committee has recently made amends by proposing to the Robbins Committee on Higher Education that Colleges of Advanced Technology 'be granted charters enabling them to bestow specified degrees....'.

CHAPTER IV

THE WORK OF THE OFFICE

'WHEN BUZZER SOUNDS'

36 Gordon Square

Callers at the headquarters of the Association of Universities of the British Commonwealth find themselves standing before a dignified but unpretentious house in Gordon Square, with a notice on the door: 'Ring top bell. When buzzer sounds enter by right door.' This is symbolic of the place, of its informality and simplicity. It is an open door for vice-chancellors, professors, lecturers, registrars and bursars from all over the Commonwealth. The overseas academic may come just to sign the visitors' book and to leave a forwarding address; or he may want to know about posts vacant in his subject; or he may want advice as to where in Britain he will find certain people or certain facilities; or he may want to try out on the Secretary some bright idea. All such services as these the secretariat willingly performs; yet it is only in its spare time (or, rather, overtime) that it performs these services, for in addition to this constant and welcome traffic of visitors the secretariat carries an astonishing burden of office work.

First of all—though it is a comparatively trivial matter—is its circulation list of these same visitors, and of many others who never come near the office. Three times a year there is circulated all over Britain a list of academic visitors from elsewhere in the Commonwealth. Each list runs to some eight hundred names; most of the names are supplied to the office by registrars of overseas universities. The lists are greatly appreciated in Britain. Many a professor, on the look-out for scholars to invite to his department (or even for potential candidates for a vacancy on his staff), uses this list to help solve his problems.

But the distribution of some eight or nine hundred copies of this, three times a year, is mere chicken-feed for the secretariat. Its really massive activities are the issue of the *Yearbook* and other publications; the appointments service; the management of two major scholarship schemes; the organization of congresses, inter-congress conferences, and the annual Home Universities Conferences; and the secretarial work for the Committee of Vice-Chancellors. No portrait of the Association would be complete without a description of these activities. Let us begin with publications.

Publications

The *Yearbook* is edited, published, and distributed from 36 Gordon Square. For the greater part of each year the staff of five in this section of the office is preparing for the next edition. Up-to-date material has to be collected from some two hundred universities and colleges in twenty-two countries. The index to the last edition of the *Yearbook* contains about fifty thousand names. The book itself is about the length of *War and Peace*; and although admittedly it is easier to write than *War and Peace*, it is incomparably more difficult to proof-read! It is a monumental achievement, repeated annually (now in an edition of over four thousand copies) in an upper room of the office to which academics rarely penetrate. There are, of course, other publications issued from this room. There are the annual reports of Home Universities Conferences, in the editing of which the staff sometimes has to exert the techniques of diplomacy to persuade some speaker that the record must contain what he said, not what he would like to have said. There is a booklet on *United Kingdom Postgraduate Awards*, re-edited every two years; and the publications staff co-operate with the British Council in producing, also every two years, *Higher Education in the United Kingdom: a Handbook for Students from Overseas*.

Naturally a section of the office with such responsibilities as these is a storehouse of information about universities and is constantly being used to deal with inquiries and queries from outside and from other parts of the office. It is the source of intelligence (in the military if not in the psychological sense of the word) not only for the rest of the office but for universities and government departments and learned societies, and it has by now assembled a very respectable reference library.

Appointments service

The raw statistics are themselves impressive. There are over five thousand inquiries a year and the Association is asked to help over something approaching nine hundred academic, research, and technical posts overseas. When the significance of the word 'help' is examined, the work of this section becomes even more impressive. For, at its maximum, 'help' means putting advertisements of an overseas vacancy into the Press, circulating detailed particulars to British universities, responding to inquiries about the advertisement, receiving applications and sending copies of them to the overseas university so that a short-list can be prepared, getting together anything up to four professors on the same day at the same time to interview short-listed candidates, bringing the candidates for interview (sometimes from overseas), paying the travel expenses of the interviewing committee and the candidate, preparing a report to go to the overseas university, and, if a candidate from Britain is appointed, probably making travel arrangements to the overseas university for himself, his family, and his furniture! Of course not all vacant posts involve all this; often all the overseas university wants the Association to do is to advertise the vacancy and to circulate particulars about it; but in 1960–1 the Association did convene in London no fewer than seventy-one advisory committees to interview applicants. It is a massive service for such a small secretariat. The cost of the service falls on those universities which use it and the charges depend on the extent to which the service is used. The importance of the service is clear from the weight of traffic it carries: in 1961–2 the bill paid by the Association for advertisements alone exceeded £39,000. This gives some measure of the volume of academic migration between Commonwealth countries.

Scholarship schemes

The Association plays a major part in the administration of two big scholarship schemes: that of the Marshall Aid Commemoration Commission, and that of the

The Work of the Office

Commonwealth Scholarship and Fellowship Plan. The Marshall Aid Commemoration Commission offers twenty-four scholarships a year to American graduates, to enable them to study for two to three years in any British university. There is a nation-wide competition in the United States for these scholarships; some 750 applications are received and the selection is made by committees of Americans in the United States. Thereafter the Marshall scholars become the responsibility of the A.U.B.C., which finds places for them in British universities, arranges their travel, meets them on arrival in Europe, pays their emoluments, arranges certain festive occasions for them, and acts *in loco parentis* towards them. As part of the brighter side of these responsibilities, the Secretary of the A.U.B.C., who is also executive secretary of the Commission, may have to attend their weddings and the christening of their first-born. As part of the more sombre side he, or his staff, may have to stand by them in adversity or counsel them in perplexity. Since at any one time there are over fifty Marshall scholars in Britain, this amounts to a considerable—though welcome—load on the secretariat of the Association.

The administration of the Commonwealth Scholarship and Fellowship Plan is—quantitatively, at any rate—an even greater responsibility. At the first Commonwealth Education Conference, held in July 1959 at Oxford, the dreams of half a century came true: a plan in the grand manner was approved for the migration of a thousand young scholars to and from all parts of the Commonwealth. Britain's share in that Plan is to bring to institutions of higher education in these islands some five hundred scholars from other parts of the Commonwealth and to recommend the names of young British scholars who wish to spend two or three years studying in Commonwealth countries outside Britain. To administer the Plan in Britain, Parliament set up a Commonwealth Scholarship Commission under the Chairmanship of the Earl of Scarbrough. The Association was asked to provide the secretariat for this Commission and to share with the British Council responsibility for carrying out the Commission's policy. It was an exciting challenge which the Association met with enthusiasm. It had to be met at once, before the interest generated at the Oxford Conference had evaporated. With the encouragement of the British government, the Association did not even wait for the Commission to be established: between September and December 1959 an Interim Committee, under the Association's Vice-Chairman, made arrangements to call for applications from all parts of the Commonwealth, invited panels of distinguished scholars and scientists in Britain to consider the applications, and set up machinery to bring the first wave of Commonwealth scholars to Britain in the autumn of 1960. The machinery worked admirably, and the Commission, which was appointed in January 1960, dealt with 452 nominations and offered scholarships to 219 candidates. The Association set up a special section of the secretariat to deal with this work. The section serves the Commission and its committees, organizes the panels which scrutinize nominations, finds places for scholars in British universities and colleges, and keeps track of the academic progress of the scholars. Within a year of its establishment, this section of the A.U.B.C. was dealing with nearly five hundred nominations from overseas (selected from nearly five thousand applications) and was placing in Britain over two hundred scholars. It has an additional duty, to compile each year for the Commonwealth Education Liaison Committee a report on the working of the whole Scholarship and Fellowship Plan. This involves the collection and integration of reports from every part of the Commonwealth. The first Report, published in 1961, is vivid evidence of the success of an operation which has its roots in the same soil as the roots of the Association: the conference held sixty years ago.[1]

There are other, smaller, scholarship and fellowship schemes which the Association helps to run: the Frank Knox Memorial fellowships to Harvard, the Drapers' Company scholarships which send British schoolboys to certain Commonwealth universities, and the Imperial Relations Trust fellowships which enable a university administrative officer from one part of the Commonwealth to spend some months in some other part.

Congresses and Conferences

The Association's work in staging quinquennial congresses and in arranging inter-congress meetings of the Executive Council has already been described. All that remains to be mentioned here are the Home Universities Conferences held on a Friday and Saturday every December, organized under the auspices of the Committee of Vice-Chancellors. These annual con-

[1] *Commonwealth Scholarship and Fellowship Plan, First Annual Report 1960–61. Second Annual Report, 1961–62.* Prepared by the A.U.B.C. for the Commonwealth Education Liaison Committee.

ferences are strictly utilitarian, without frills or entertainment. They are a useful occasion for an exchange of ideas (very often old and well-worn ideas) about the perennial topics of talk in faculty boards and common-rooms. One great advantage of them is that the predominant voices are those of scholars and scientists, not university administrators. Through them, the A.U.B.C. does for the universities of Britain what is done, through congresses, for the universities of the Commonwealth.

Secretariat of the Committee of Vice-Chancellors and Principals

Chapter III gives a bird's-eye view, as it were, of the origin and work of this remarkable Committee. Here we are concerned with the worm's-eye view: what does responsibility for this Committee mean to the secretariat? The Committee meets once a month on a Friday. On the Friday a week beforehand a massive agenda and supporting papers go out to the members. At 10.30 the Committee assembles in a chamber of somewhat austere and gloomy dignity in the Senate House of London University. The Committee sits till lunch-time, and occasionally reassembles in the afternoon. Much of the business is highly technical: academic salaries, the rating of university buildings, salary scales for technicians, superannuation arrangements, entrance requirements, negotiations over Anglo-German or Anglo-French conferences. The senior secretaries take notes and clarify the action the Committee wishes to take. A lady secretary, making a shorthand record of what is said, vanishes at mid-morning to type it out, to be succeeded by another lady secretary who continues the shorthand record until lunch-time. A week after the meeting, on the next Friday, very full minutes go out to each member of the Committee. Also in that week following the meeting dozens of letters or circulars will have been posted to universities on matters arising out of the meeting, and the Chairman will have dictated letters to the University Grants Committee and to other bodies whose activities concern the universities. In addition to all this there are meetings of sub-committees (such as those which deal with questions of academic salaries, technicians' salaries, pensions, and rating), and in recent years there has been a succession of publications from the Committee, too.

Antecedents to Gordon Square

These, then, are some of the activities which go on at 36 Gordon Square and in the premises, recently acquired for part of the Association's work, in Marlborough House. And yet there is no smell of formality or bureaucracy about the office. Visitors have easy access to the Secretary himself, and the Secretary not only presides over all these activities, but has to spend a great deal of his time on meetings outside: with the British Council, the Fulbright Commission, the British Institute in Paris, and the International Association of Universities (which contrives to meet in romantic and remote spots like Istanbul and Mexico City).

How is the atmosphere of informality preserved? Largely through the traditions of the Association, which its present secretariat wisely cherishes. The Association began in a room in the Imperial Institute. In its early days all its business was done by a voluntary secretary and a lady clerk. It has never aspired to those two deadly solvents of informality: size and power; and if it ever did have such aspirations the universities which support it would soon intervene. And so, although there is now a total staff of thirty-nine (small enough in all conscience for this traffic of work) the office remains a family rather than a hierarchy.

Let us glance backwards for a moment at the antecedents to 36 Gordon Square. Until the end of the First World War there was no real office, simply one borrowed room in the Imperial Institute. At the end of the war the Bureau (as it then was) acquired a house—50 Russell Square—with a grant from the government. The circumstances of this purchase are described on pages 24–6. There the office remained from 1919 to 1930, when it migrated to 88*a* Gower Street. In September 1940 it was forcibly dislodged from this home by a German bomb (which destroyed many of the records). Again it became the guest of another Institution: this time University College, London, itself badly bombed, acted as host to the office until 1946. Then it had a succession of temporary homes until 1955: 24 Gordon Square (1946), 8 Park Street (1947), 32 Woburn Square (1948), and 5 Gordon Square (1949). In 1955 the Association moved into 36 Gordon Square which remains its headquarters,[1] a house which is well on the

[1] The Association owes its post-war accommodation both at 5 Gordon Square and at 36–37 Gordon Square to the University of London. Moreover the lease of the Association's present premises is substantially longer than that which the University normally grants to its tenants and the rent is at a concessionary rate. Indeed, the Association is in debt to the University of London for a series of acts of goodwill throughout its whole history since 1912.

way to becoming 'the Mecca' (as Sir James Barrett said forty-eight years ago) 'of every University man in the Dominions'. Very recently (1961) the Association has opened a branch office in Marlborough House, a royal residence presented to the nation for use as a Commonwealth Centre in Britain. Here, very appropriately, are to be found those sections of the office which deal with Commonwealth scholarships and overseas appointments.

The office has been fortunate in its secretaries, and it is due to them that it has so admirably combined efficiency with informality. Brief biographical notes about them appear in Appendix VIII. For six years (1913–19) Alex Hill acted as Honorary Secretary and combined the work with his Principalship of University College, Southampton; then for another ten years (1919–29) he served full-time as Secretary. He was succeeded for a year by Frank Heath (1929–30) who transformed the office from being a 'one man show', not adapted for growth, into an organization which, though still small, could grow. In 1930 he was succeeded by W. B. Brander (formerly of the Indian Civil Service) who was in charge for seventeen years, until 1947. After the Second World War, as after the First, the Bureau (as it was still called) was offered exciting opportunities to promote Commonwealth cohesion. Its present Secretary, J. F. Foster, who followed Brander and who was formerly Registrar of the University of Melbourne, came in time to seize these opportunities, and the present high standing of the Association with universities and with governments is due largely to his energy and vision.

7-2

CHAPTER V

THE
COMMUNITY OF COMMONWEALTH
UNIVERSITIES

The balance sheet for British colonialism includes four substantial assets: Christianity, representative government, educational institutions and the English language. Of course not all parts of the Commonwealth have drawn equally upon all these assets. Countries virtually empty of indigenous civilization, such as Australia and Canada, have made use of them all. Countries with ancient and venerable religions have made less use than others of Christianity; countries with a sophisticated indigenous language and literature have made less use than others of the English tongue. Representative government has been transplanted to them all, but in some Commonwealth countries it has had to be greatly changed to meet local needs. Of these four assets the most universally acceptable, and the least changed by the indigenous cultural environment, are the educational institutions exported from Britain to her Commonwealth. Of course educational institutions are no monopoly of Europe: there were madrasas and Koranic schools in the Moslem world long before European education arrived. There were institutions for higher education in India nine centuries before teaching began in Oxford. But by a process of natural selection among social institutions, the European pattern of school and university has firmly established itself, and has even displaced ancient educational institutions deeply rooted in the indigenous culture. This is a world-wide pheno-menon: Al-Azhar in Cairo, one of the most ancient institutions of higher education in the world, which has for centuries attracted scholars from as far east as Indonesia and as far west as Morocco, is now to be metamorphosed into a university with schools of medicine, business administration and engineering; and it is three generations since the daigaku of Japan became transformed into a university.

The export of higher education from Britain began over three hundred years ago when John Harvard, from Emmanuel College, Cambridge, left his property to the College just opened in Massachusetts, and Henry Dunster, from Magdalene College, Cambridge, was appointed President of the College. Since then uni-versities modelled on those in Britain have been established all over the Commonwealth.[1] Scottish universities greatly influenced Dalhousie and McGill and Queen's in Canada. London University provided the pattern which F. J. Mouat used for his 'pro-posed plan of the University of Calcutta' which was a prototype for universities in India.[2] Sydney University

[1] Of course Britain is by no means the only European country which has exported universities. In Canada the universities of Laval and Montreal were inspired from France, and in recent times the French university has been exported to Senegal. Salamanca was the model for universities in Mexico and Peru, and a non-European pattern—the American State university—was the model for universities in the Philippines, Puerto Rico and Eastern Nigeria.

[2] For a discussion of the origin of universities in India and Africa, see E. Ashby, *Patterns of Universities in Non-European Societies.* School of Oriental and African Studies (London, 1961).

drew on London and (under the influence of its first professors) on the ancient universities of England for its initial inspiration. And more recently the university colleges in tropical Africa—now becoming full universities—were established as close replicas of modern English civic universities like those at Nottingham and Hull.

Transplanted universities do not indefinitely remain replicas of the stock from which they come. Harvard is unlike Cambridge. McGill is unlike Edinburgh. The universities of India and Australia have departed a long way from the University of London. Like vegetation adapted to alps and deserts, universities adapt themselves to unfamiliar environments. Yet they remain unmistakably universities; notwithstanding local differences in emphasis, they pursue similar curricula; they aspire to remain on a 'gold standard' of scholarship; none of them could stand alone and their strength lies in the fact that they share a common tradition and they draw freely on one another's resources. It is common knowledge that the most recent additions to the Commonwealth's academic family, the universities of tropical Africa, have a high proportion of expatriate staff. But it is not so commonly known that, among the non-medical professors in a university as mature as Sydney, more than half took their first degrees in universities outside Australasia; more than half the professors in Wellington took their first degrees outside New Zealand; and the staff of Manchester University includes teachers who graduated from universities in Australia, Canada, India and New Zealand, beside others from no less than fourteen foreign countries.[1] It is no wonder that the universities of the Commonwealth—indeed of the whole Western world—are held together in an undefined but indivisible society.

If we allow this society to lose its cohesion it will disintegrate, and if it disintegrates we shall have lost one of the most powerful forces uniting the countries of the Commonwealth; for Commonwealth leadership is largely in the hands of graduates, and, by virtue of the cohesion among Commonwealth universities, graduates from as far apart as Singapore and Vancouver, Ghana and Aberdeen, find that they share common assumptions, common cultural traditions, common canons of criticism and facility in using a common language. If the society is to remain healthy and to preserve its cohesion, the channels of communication between its members must be kept open and free for traffic. There is of course a great deal of direct communication through the circulation of learned journals and the exchange of off-prints. But not only ideas, men too, must be in circulation. Several agencies contribute to this essential traffic. The great foundations are generous in providing money for travel and study leave. There is, for instance, a whole programme of the Carnegie Corporation of New York devoted to travel grants for university teachers in Commonwealth countries outside Britain, and the Nuffield Foundation has a somewhat similar scheme. Governments of various Commonwealth countries help,

[1] Austria. Belgium, China, Czechoslovakia, Denmark, Germany, Italy, Palestine, Poland, South Africa, Spain, Switzerland, U.S.A. and U.S.S.R.

too: at any one time the British Council sponsors and assists about 1500 Commonwealth overseas visitors to Britain and the new Commonwealth Scholarship and Fellowship scheme (described on page 85) is creating an impressive network of exchange not just between Britain and her sister-countries, but among the sister-countries themselves.

In this task of keeping open the channels of communication between Commonwealth universities, of preserving cohesion among the members of this unique society of learning, of safeguarding the integrity of the idea of a university, the Association of Universities of the British Commonwealth plays a major part. It is difficult now to imagine how Commonwealth universities would get on without the Association: without its *Yearbook*, its appointments service, its quinquennial congresses.

Indeed the importance of the Association is not likely to diminish, but to increase. For Commonwealth countries inevitably undergo changes in personality; they diverge more and more from the metropolitan image. Australia, for instance, while preserving some features of its colonial days, has modified others, rejected still others, and added unique features of its own. Nothing is more certain than that similar changes will occur in the newer Commonwealth countries. The Commonwealth family will continually diversify. It therefore becomes of prime importance to promote a free trade in ideas, and of men who specialize in ideas, between Commonwealth countries. This is most easily done through their universities. The Association's task, as it enters upon its second half century, is to facilitate this free trade. Fortunately its first half century qualifies it for this task, for, as this book has shown, the Association has always remained independent of governments and disengaged from politics. It belongs to its member-universities and it embodies their ideals of co-operation in the world of scholarship.

HOME UNIVERSITIES COMMITTEE FOR THE 1912 CONGRESS

Sir Edward Busk, Chairman of Convocation of the University of London.

Sir William J. Collins, Vice-Chancellor of the University of London.

Sir Alfred Dale, Vice-Chancellor of the University of Liverpool.

Sir James Donaldson, Vice-Chancellor and Principal of the University of St Andrews.

Sir Charles Eliot, Vice-Chancellor of the University of Sheffield.

Rev. T. C. Fitzpatrick, President of Queens' College, Cambridge.

Rev. Thomas Hamilton, Vice-Chancellor and President of the Queen's University of Belfast.

C. B. Heberden, Vice-Chancellor of the University of Oxford; Principal of Brasenose College, Oxford.

Sir Alfred Hopkinson, Vice-Chancellor of the Victoria University of Manchester.

Sir Oliver Lodge, Principal of the University of Birmingham.

Sir Donald MacAlister, Vice-Chancellor and Principal of the University of Glasgow.

R. W. Macan, Master of University College, Oxford.

Rev. Canon A. J. Mason, Master of Pembroke College, Cambridge.

Sir Henry A. Miers, Principal of the University of London.

Sir Christopher Nixon, Vice-Chancellor of the National University of Ireland.

Sir Isambard Owen, Vice-Chancellor of the University of Bristol.

Sir George Hare Philipson, Vice-Chancellor of the University of Durham.

Sir Harry R. Reichel, Vice-Chancellor of the University of Wales.

Michael E. Sadler, Vice-Chancellor of the University of Leeds.

Appendix I

R. F. Scott, Vice-Chancellor of the University of Cambridge; Master of St John's College, Cambridge.

Rev. G. Adam Smith, Vice-Chancellor and Principal of the University of Aberdeen.

Anthony Traill, Provost of Trinity College, Dublin.

Sir William Turner, Vice-Chancellor and Principal of the University of Edinburgh.

Professor T. H. Warren, President of Magdalen College, Oxford.

CONGRESS OF THE UNIVERSITIES OF THE EMPIRE, 1912

Universities Represented[1]

(1) *The United Kingdom*

ENGLAND AND WALES

University of Birmingham
University of Bristol
University of Cambridge
University of Durham
University of Leeds
University of Liverpool
University of London
Victoria University of
  Manchester
University of Oxford
University of Sheffield
University of Wales

SCOTLAND

University of Aberdeen
University of Edinburgh
University of Glasgow
University of St Andrews

IRELAND

Queen's University, Belfast
University of Dublin
National University of
  Ireland

(2) *The Dominions and Colonies*

AUSTRALIA

University of Adelaide
University of Melbourne
University of Queensland
University of Sydney
University of Tasmania
University of Western
  Australia

NEW ZEALAND

University of New Zealand

SOUTH AFRICA

University of the Cape of
  Good Hope

CHINA

University of Hong Kong

EUROPE

University of Malta

CANADA

Ontario

  McMaster University,
    Toronto
University of Ottawa
Queen's University, Kingston
University of Toronto
  Trinity, Toronto
  Victoria, Toronto
Western University, London

Appendix II

CANADA (*cont.*)

Quebec

University of Bishop's
College, Lennoxville

Laval University, Quebec
and Montreal

McGill University, Montreal

New Brunswick

University of New Brunswick, Fredericton

University of Mount
Allison, Sackville

Nova Scotia

Acadia University, Wolfville

Dalhousie University, Halifax

Nova Scotia (*cont.*)

University of King's College,
Windsor

University of St Francis
Xavier, Antigonish

Alberta

University of Alberta

Saskatchewan

University of Saskatchewan

Manitoba

University of Manitoba

British Columbia

University of British
Columbia

(3) *India*

University of Allahabad

University of Bombay

University of Calcutta

University of Madras

Panjab University, Lahore

¹ As set out in the *Report of Proceedings, Congress of the Universities of the Empire*, 1912, pp. xii–xiii.

NUMBERS OF MEMBER INSTITUTIONS, 1932–62

(NOTE. *During 1931, the first year of operation under the new Articles of Association in which corporate membership of the Bureau was introduced, forty-six universities became ordinary members.*)

Year	Ordinary	Associate	Additional	Total
1932–3	50	6	—	56
1933–4	49	6	1	56
1934–5	48	6	1	55
1935–6	47	6	1	54
1936–7	46	6	1	53
1937–8	46	8	1	55
1938–9	46	8	1	55
1939–40	46	8	1	55
1940–1	46	8	1	55
1941–2	44	8	4	56
1942–3	44	8	4	56
1943–4	43	10	4	57
1944–5	45	10	4	59
1945–6	45	12	4	61
1946–7	41	12	4	57
1947–8	47	12	4	63
1948–9	53	12	4	69
1949–50	57	16	3	76
1950–1	64	17	3	84
1951–2	74	16	3	93
1952–3	86	16	5	107
1953–4	90	16	4	110
1954–5	91	16	3	110
1955–6	94	15	3	112
1956–7	96	15	3	114
1957–8	100	15	4	119
1958–9	102	15	4	121
1959–60	103	17	4	124
1960–1	103	15	4	122
1961–2	118	10	4	132

SUMMARY OF FINANCES

(1) Period before incorporation (1913–19)

	£
Total of contributions from 29 member universities	2398
Total expenditure	2401

(2) Period after incorporation and before separation of accounts according to functions (1920–49)[1]

		Income (£)	Expenditure (£)
Quinquennium	1921–5	14,848	14,113
	1925–30	15,494	14,507
	1930–5	22,034	17,983
	1935–40	21,844	21,444
	1940–5	20,040	12,351
Four years	1945–9	35,772	34,172

(3) Period after separation of accounts into 'General' (for all member institutions), 'Committee of Vice-Chancellors and Principals' (for U.K. universities), and 'Appointments work' (for various overseas universities) (1949–62)

		Income (£)	Expenditure (£)
Quinquennium 1949–54:			
General		38,078	34,561
U.K. universities		43,560	27,680
Appointments		11,586	20,657
	Total	£93,224	£82,898
Quinquennium 1954–9:			
General		67,175	62,215
U.K. universities		62,069	54,579
Appointments		37,007	31,481
	Total	£166,251	£148,275
Three years 1959–62:			
General		89,044	101,720
U.K. universities		41,481	37,944
Appointments		47,727	27,894
	Total	£178,252	£167,558

[1] The figures for 1921–35 are taken from the table facing page 246 in the Report of the 1936 Congress. The figures for 1935–49 are taken from the printed accounts; they refer to financial years running from 1 August 1935 to 31 July 1949

CHAIRMEN, VICE-CHAIRMEN, HON. TREASURERS AND SECRETARIES, 1913–63

(Described by the titles which they held during their period of office. The prefix † indicates that they were subsequently knighted.)

CHAIRMAN	Period of service
Sir Donald MacAlister, Vice-Chancellor and Principal, University of Glasgow	1913–21
Sir George Adam Smith, Vice-Chancellor and Principal, University of Aberdeen	1921–6
Sir Harry R. Reichel, Vice-Chancellor, University of Wales, and Principal, University College of North Wales, Bangor	1926–9
†Dr T. Franklin Sibly, Vice-Chancellor, University of Reading	1929–34
†Dr Will Spens, Master, Corpus Christi College, Cambridge	1934–8
Sir John Stopford, Vice-Chancellor, University of Manchester	1938–43
Dr Thomas Loveday, Vice-Chancellor, University of Bristol	1943–6
The Rt Hon. Lord Harlech, Pro-Chancellor, University of Wales	1946–9
Professor Ian A. Gordon, Vice-Chancellor, University of New Zealand	1949–50
Sir A. L. Mudaliar, Vice-Chancellor, University of Madras	1950–2
Sir Philip Morris, Vice-Chancellor, University of Bristol	1952–3
Dr W. A. Mackintosh, Vice-Chancellor and Principal, Queen's University at Kingston	1953–4

Appendix V

	Period of service
Dr A. P. Rowe, Vice-Chancellor, University of Adelaide	1954–5
†Dr Robert Aitken, Vice-Chancellor and Principal, University of Birmingham	1955–6
Dr M. Raziuddin Siddiqi, Vice-Chancellor, University of Peshawar	1956–7
Dr Andrew Stewart, President, University of Alberta	1957–8
Dr T. Alty, Vice-Chancellor and Principal, Rhodes University	1958–60
†Dr Lindsay Ride, Vice-Chancellor, University of Hong Kong	1960–1
Mr K. J. Maidment, Vice-Chancellor, University of Auckland	1961–2
Sir Douglas Logan, Principal, University of London	1962–

VICE-CHAIRMAN

†Mr Harold Claughton, Principal, University of London	1946–7
Sir Raymond Priestley, Vice-Chancellor and Principal, University of Birmingham	1947–51
Sir Philip Morris, Vice-Chancellor, University of Bristol	{ 1951–2 1953–5
†Dr Robert Aitken, Vice-Chancellor and Principal, University of Birmingham	{ 1955 1956–8
Sir Eric Ashby, Vice-Chancellor, the Queen's University, Belfast; subsequently Master of Clare College, Cambridge	1958–61
Sir Douglas Logan, Principal, University of London	1961–2

TREASURER/HON. TREASURER

Treasurer

Sir Henry A. Miers	1913–18
Sir E. Cooper Perry	1918–26
Dr Peter Giles	1926–9
†Dr Edwin Deller	1929–32

Appendix V

	Period of service
Hon. Treasurer	
Sir Edwin Deller	1932–6
Sir Franklin Sibly	1937–8
Dr William Cullen	1938–48
Sir William Hamilton Fyfe	1948–54
Sir George Allen	1954–61
Professor R. Ogilvie Buchanan	1961–

HON. SECRETARY/SECRETARY

Hon. Secretary

Dr Alex Hill   1913–19

Secretary

Dr Alex Hill	1919–29
*Sir Frank Heath	1929–30
Mr W. B. Brander	1930–47
Dr J. F. Foster	1947–

* Continued as Hon. Director, 1930–4.

CONGRESSES AND INTER-CONGRESS MEETINGS

COMMONWEALTH CONGRESSES, 1912–63

Congress of the Universities of the Empire	July 1912	London
Second Congress of the Universities of the Empire	July 1921	Oxford
Third Congress of the Universities of the Empire	July 1926	Cambridge
Fourth Congress of the Universities of the Empire	July 1931	London and Edinburgh
Fifth Quinquennial Congress of the Universities of the British Empire	July 1936	Cambridge
Sixth Quinquennial Congress of the Universities of the British Common-wealth	July 1948	Oxford
Seventh Quinquennial Congress of the Universities of the Commonwealth	July 1953	Cambridge
Eighth Quinquennial Congress of the Universities of the Commonwealth	September 1958	Montreal
Ninth Quinquennial Congress of the Universities of the Commonwealth	July 1963	London

OVERSEAS MEETINGS OF THE EXECUTIVE COUNCIL, 1949–62[1]

June 1949	Canada (Halifax)
August 1950	New Zealand (Wairakei)
December 1951–January 1952	India (Madras)
September 1954	Canada (Kingston)

[1] In all countries except Hong Kong visiting members of the Executive Council toured university institutions and took part in inter-university conferences held in centres other than those where meetings of the Council took place. After the Hong Kong meeting, members of the Council visited the University of Malaya.

Appendix VI

August 1955	Australia (Melbourne)
December 1956–January 1957	Pakistan (Lahore)
April 1960	South Africa (Grahamstown and Johannesburg)
January 1961	Hong Kong
August 1962	New Zealand (Auckland, Wairakei and Wellington)

CHAIRMEN OF THE COMMITTEE OF VICE-CHANCELLORS AND PRINCIPALS, 1918–63

(Described by the titles which they held during their period of office. The prefix † indicates that they were subsequently knighted.)

Sir Donald MacAlister, Vice-Chancellor and Principal, University of Glasgow	1918–29
Sir Charles Grant Robertson, Vice-Chancellor and Principal, University of Birmingham	1929–35
Dr Thomas Loveday, Vice-Chancellor, University of Bristol	1935–8
Sir Franklin Sibly, Vice-Chancellor, University of Reading	1938–43
Sir Hector Hetherington, Vice-Chancellor and Principal, University of Glasgow	1943–7
†Professor David Hughes Parry, Vice-Chancellor, University of London	1947–8
†Dr James Mountford, Vice-Chancellor, University of Liverpool	1948–9 (May)
Sir Hector Hetherington (*Acting Chairman*)	May–September 1949
Sir Hector Hetherington	1949–52
Sir Charles Morris, Vice-Chancellor, University of Leeds	1952–5
Sir Philip Morris, Vice-Chancellor, University of Bristol	1955–8
Sir Robert Aitken, Vice-Chancellor and Principal, University of Birmingham	1958–61
Professor W. Mansfield Cooper, Vice-Chancellor, University of Manchester	1961–

BIOGRAPHICAL SUMMARIES

Arthur James Balfour, 1st Earl of Balfour (cr. 1922), K.G. (1922),
P.C., O.M. (1916), 1848–1930

Conservative M.P. almost continuously from 1874, P.C. from
1885. President of Local Government Board, 1885–6. Secretary
for Scotland, 1886–7. Chief Secretary for Ireland, 1887. Leader
of the House of Commons and First Lord of the Treasury, 1891–2
and 1895–1902. Prime Minister, 1902–5. Leader of the Opposition, 1906–11. First Lord of the Admiralty, 1915. Foreign
Secretary, 1916–19. Head of the Diplomatic Mission to America,
1917. Lord President of the Council 1919–22 and 1925–9.
Delegate to the Washington Naval Conference, 1921–2. Lord
Rector, University of St Andrews, 1886. Lord Rector, University
of Glasgow, 1890. Chancellor, University of Edinburgh, 1891 and
University of Cambridge, 1919. Sometime Gifford Lecturer,
Glasgow and Romanes Lecturer, Oxford. President of the British
Association, 1904 and the British Academy, 1921–8. Founded the
Committee of Civil Research. B. Scotland. Ed. Trinity College,
Cambridge.

Lieut.-Colonel Sir James (William) Barrett, K.B.E. (1918), C.B.
(1918), C.M.G. (1911), late R.A.M.C. and A.A.M.C., 1862–
1945

Vice-Chancellor, University of Melbourne, 1931–4, Chancellor,
1935–9. An eminent oculist and aurist who held a number of
medical appointments and served in the R.A.M.C. and A.A.M.C.
during the War of 1914–18. Lieut.-Colonel R.A.M.C., 1916.
President of the British Medical Association, 1935–6. B. Australia.
Ed. University of Melbourne and King's College, London.

William Browne Brander, C.I.E. (1927), C.B.E. (1918), 1880–1951

Secretary, Universities Bureau of the British Empire, 1930–47.
Formerly in the Indian Civil Service, 1904–31, rising to be Chief
Secretary to the Government of Burma, and Chairman of the
Development Trust, Rangoon. B. Scotland. Ed. Universities of
Edinburgh and Oxford.

Appendix VIII

William Macbride Childs, J.P., 1869–1939

First Vice-Chancellor of the University of Reading, having been Principal of the University College of Reading, 1903–26 and Vice-Principal, 1900–3, and a Lecturer from 1893, when it was a University Extension College. B. England. Ed. Keble College, Oxford.

Sir Robert (Alexander) Falconer, K.C.M.G. (1917), 1867–1943

President of the University of Toronto, 1907–32. Formerly a Professor at and then Principal (1904–7) of Pine Hill Presbyterian Theological College, Halifax, N.S. President, Royal Society of Canada, 1931–2, Royal Canadian Institute, 1933–5, Champlain Society, 1937–42. B. Canada. Ed. Queen's Royal College School, Trinidad, London and Edinburgh Universities; also studied at Leipzig, Berlin and Marburg.

Herbert Albert Laurens Fisher, O.M. (1937), 1865–1940

Warden of New College, Oxford, 1925–40. M.P. for Hallam, 1916–18 and for the Combined English Universities, 1918–26. President of the Board of Education, 1916–22. Vice-Chancellor of the University of Sheffield, 1912–16. Served on Royal Commission on Public Services in India, 1912–17. President of the British Academy, 1928–32. B. England. Ed. New College, Oxford and Göttingen and Paris.

Sir (Thomas) Gregory Foster, Bt. (1930), Kt. (1917), 1866–1931

Vice-Chancellor, University of London, 1928–30. Provost of University College, London, 1904–29. Secretary, University College, London and Assistant Professor, 1900–4. Professor of English, Bedford College, London, 1897–1900. B. England. Ed. University College, London, and Strasbourg.

Sir (Henry) Frank Heath, G.B.E. (1927), K.C.B. (1917), C.B. (1911), 1863–1946

Secretary, Universities Bureau of the British Empire, 1929–30 and Hon. Director, 1930–4. First Permanent Secretary to the Department of Scientific and Industrial Research, 1916–27. Secretary to the Advisory Council for Scientific and Industrial Research, 1915–27. Director, Office of special inquiries and reports, Board of Education, 1903–16 and Principal Assistant Secretary of the Universities Branch of the Board, 1910–16. Member of the Treasury Advisory Committee on Grants to

University Colleges, 1909–11. Education Correspondent to the Government of India, 1904–16. Joint Secretary to the Royal Commission on University Education in London, 1909–13. Academic Registrar and Acting Treasurer, University of London, 1901–3 and Assistant Registrar and Librarian, 1895–1901. Professor of English, Bedford College, London, 1890–5 and lecturer, King's College, London, 1891–5. Member of numerous other committees and commissions. B. England. Ed. University College, London, and Strasbourg.

Alex Hill, O.B.E., J.P., 1856–1929

Secretary, Universities Bureau of the British Empire, 1913–29. Organizing Secretary, First Congress of the Universities of the Empire, 1911–12. Principal, University College, Southampton, 1912–19. Master of Downing College, 1888–1907 and Vice-Chancellor, University of Cambridge, 1897–9. Professor, Royal College of Surgeons, 1884–5. President of the Neurological Society and of the Teachers' Guild of Great Britain. B. England. Ed. Downing College, Cambridge and St Bartholomew's Hospital, London.

Sir Thomas (Henry) Holland, K.C.S.I. (1918), K.C.I.E. (1908), 1868–1947

Principal and Vice-Chancellor, University of Edinburgh, 1929–44. Rector, Imperial College of Science and Technology, University of London, 1922–9. Formerly in the Indian Civil Service—from 1890 holding the following appointments: Director, Geological Survey of India (1903–10); President, Indian Industrial Commission (1916); President of the Indian Munitions Board (1917); Member, Viceroy's Executive Council (1920–1). Professor of Geology, Victoria University of Manchester, 1910–18. President of many societies and institutions. B. England. Ed. Royal School of Mines, South Kensington.

John William Joynt, 1852–1933

Representative in England of the University of New Zealand, 1910–31. Member of the Executive Committee of the Universities Bureau of the British Empire from 1913. Formerly Registrar, University of New Zealand; Lecturer, Victoria University College, Wellington and Principal of Nelson College, New Zealand. B. Ireland, went to New Zealand for health reasons. Ed. Trinity College, Dublin.

Appendix VIII

Sir Donald MacAlister, Bt. (1924), K.C.B. (1908), 1854–1934

Principal and Vice-Chancellor of University of Glasgow, 1907–29, and Chancellor, 1929–34. First Chairman of the Standing Committee of Vice-Chancellors and Principals, 1918–29. First Chairman of the Universities Bureau of the British Empire, 1913. Chairman of Delegates, Congress of the Universities of the British Empire, 1912, 1921 and 1926. Formerly lecturer and physician in Cambridge. President of the General Medical Council, 1904–31. (Served on numerous commissions and held many other appointments.) B. Scotland. Ed. St John's College, Cambridge and St Bartholomew's Hospital, London, and Leipzig.

Sir William (Symington) McCormick, G.B.E. (1929), Kt. (1911), 1859–1930

First Chairman of the University Grants Committee, 1919–30, having been a member of the precursors of this Committee from 1906 and Chairman from 1911. Chairman of the Advisory Council on Scientific and Industrial Research, 1915. Secretary to the Carnegie Trust for the Universities of Scotland, 1901. Formerly Professor of English Literature, University College, Dundee, and lecturer, University of St Andrews. B. Scotland. Ed. Universities of Glasgow, Göttingen, and Marburg.

Sir Henry (Alexander) Miers, Kt. (1912), 1858–1942

Vice-Chancellor, Victoria University of Manchester and Professor of Crystallography, 1915–26. Principal, University of London, 1908–15. Waynflete Professor of Mineralogy, Oxford, 1895–1908. Fellow and (1902–3) President of Magdalen College. B. Brazil. Ed. Eton and Trinity College, Oxford, and studied at Strasbourg.

John Ramsay Bryce Muir (1872–1941)

Professor of Modern History, Victoria University of Manchester, 1913–21. Member of the Sadler Commission, 1917–19. Professor of Modern History, University of Liverpool, 1906–13, and lecturer, 1899–1906. Liberal M.P. for Rochdale, 1923–4. Chairman of the Organizing Committee of the Liberal Party, 1930–1. Chairman of the National Liberal Federation, 1931–3 and President, 1933–6. Vice-President of the Liberal Party Organization, 1936–41. B. England. Ed. University College, Liverpool and Balliol College, Oxford.

Appendix VIII

Sir (Horatio) Gilbert (George) Parker, P.C., Bt. (1915), 1862–1932

Initiator and organizer of the first Allied Colonial Universities Conference, 1903. M.P. for Gravesend, 1900–18. In charge of American publicity for 2½ years during the War of 1914–18. Chairman of the Imperial South African Association, 1903–11. Chairman and founder of the Small Ownership Committee and Chairman of the Government Overseas Committee. Associate editor of the *Sydney Herald*, 1885. B. Canada. Ed. Trinity College, Toronto.

Sir George (Robert) Parkin, K.G.M.G. (1920), 1846–1922

First organizing Secretary of the Rhodes Scholarship Trust, 1902–20. Principal of Upper Canada College, Toronto, 1895–1902. Headmaster of Collegiate School, Fredericton, 1871–89 and Gloucester Grammar School, Bathurst, 1867–71. Worked for the cause of the Imperial Federation League, 1889–95. B. Canada. Ed. University of New Brunswick and studied at Oxford.

Robert Davies Roberts, J.P., 1851–1911

Organizing Secretary for the First Congress of the Universities of the British Empire, 1910–11. First Registrar of the Extension Board of the University of London, 1902–11. Chairman, Executive Committee, University of Wales, 1910–11. Junior Deputy Chancellor, University of Wales, 1903–5. Secretary to the London Society for the Extension of University Teaching, 1885–1904. In charge of the Cambridge Syndicate for University Extension, 1894–1902. Secretary to the Gilchrist Trust, 1899–1911. High Sheriff of Cardiganshire, 1902–3. B. Wales. Ed. University College, London, and Clare College, Cambridge.

Sir Michael (Ernest) Sadler, K.C.S.I. (1919), C.B. (1911), 1861–1943

Master of University College, Oxford, 1923–34. Vice-Chancellor, University of Leeds, 1911–23. President of the Commission on the University of Calcutta (Sadler Commission), 1917–19. Professor of Education, Victoria University of Manchester, 1903–11. Director, Office of special inquiries and reports, Department of Education, 1895–1903. Inspired and was a member of the Royal Commission on Secondary Education, 1893. Secretary of Extension Lecturers' Sub-Committee of the Oxford University Examinations Delegacy, 1885–95. B. England. Ed. Trinity College, Oxford.

Appendix VIII

Sir (Thomas) Franklin Sibly, K.B.E. (1943), Kt. (1938), 1883–1948

Vice-Chancellor of the University of Reading, 1929–46. Chairman of the Committee of Vice-Chancellors and Principals, 1938–43. Chairman of the Executive Committee and Council of the Universities Bureau of the British Empire, 1929–34. Principal, University of London, 1926–9. Vice-Chancellor, University of Wales, 1925–6. First Principal of University College, Swansea, 1920–6. Professor at Armstrong College, Newcastle, 1918–20, and at University College, Cardiff, 1913–18. Lecturer, King's College, London, 1908–13. Chairman of the Geological Survey Board, 1930–43. Member of the Advisory Council of the Department of Scientific and Industrial Research, 1932–7 and 1941–6. B. England. Ed. University College, Bristol.

Henry Marshall Tory, 1864–1947

Member of the Executive Committee of the Universities Bureau of the British Empire, 1912–26. President, University of Alberta, 1908–28. Member of the Imperial Education Committee. President, National Research Council of Canada, 1923–35 and Director, National Research Laboratories, 1927–35. President, Royal Society of Canada, 1938–39. President, Carlton College, Ottawa, 1943. Served on many commissions; formerly Lecturer and Fellow of McGill University. Ed. McGill and Cambridge.

INDEX

Index